The invisible painting

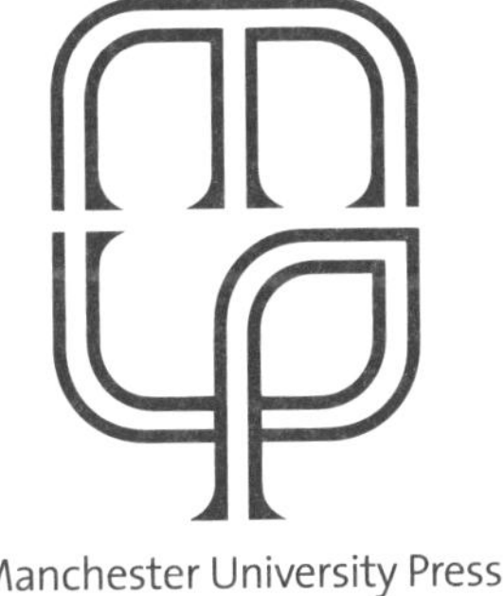

Manchester University Press

The invisible painting
My memoir of Leonora Carrington

Gabriel Weisz Carrington

Manchester University Press

Published by Manchester University Press
Oxford Road, Manchester M13 9PL

www.manchesteruniversitypress.co.uk

British Library Cataloguing-in-Publication Data
A catalogue record for this book is available from the British Library

ISBN   978 1 5261 5393 7   hardback
ISBN   978 1 5261 6964 8   paperback

First published 2021
Paperback published 2023

The publisher has no responsibility for the persistence or accuracy of URLs for any external or third-party internet websites referred to in this book, and does not guarantee that any content on such websites is, or will remain, accurate or appropriate.

Typeset by
Servis Filmsetting Ltd, Stockport, Cheshire
Printed in Great Britain by
Bell & Bain Ltd, Glasgow

Contents

Preface

Jonathan P. Eburne

I first met Gabriel Weisz at a scholarly conference in 2009. Then, as now, I was struck by his majestic eyebrows, which rise up like bats' wings from their perch above his eyes. I also found it impossible to ignore his singular manner of punctuating phrases: in place of the overused affirmative, he parses each phrase with a negative question. It makes for a strong impression, no?

I was also, and remain, transfixed by his kindness and intellectual hunger.

Gabriel Weisz, like his late mother, Leonora Carrington, is a scholar of fantastic literature and its animating tendencies: philosophy, magic, shamanism, becoming-animal. In addition to his published writings on the arts, sciences, and cultures of transformation, he has also published poetry and drama and, in recent years, has become a writer of memoirs as well. I can hear his voice in my head as I read the pages of *The invisible painting*; I hope you can hear it too. It is a memorable voice.

Gabriel Weisz, also like his late mother, is something of a shamanic figure himself – a statement which, as I write it, rings false. Perhaps it would be more accurate to say that for someone who lives at the very borders of myth, who straddles the realms of quotidian existence and magic, Gabriel is startlingly, almost shockingly, *normal*. He and his partner, Paty Argomedo, go to the shops; they wash the dishes; they run the vacuum cleaner. When they travel abroad they carry their passports and papers in theft-proof document purses slung beneath their clothes. Paty and Gabriel are generous hosts, correspondents, interlocutors; they are doting parents.

Again I stop myself, for in portraying Gabriel this way I am still missing something, once again lapsing into falsification. It occurs to me that for such an allegedly normal person – 'normal' being a term that Gabriel, a child of Surrealism, would hold in absolute contempt – Gabriel Weisz is also deeply, deliciously weird. How grateful I am for this.

'To those who live in emotional poverty', Gabriel writes in the pages that follow, 'other people's happiness can be perceived as a threat.' The wisdom in this observation lies at the heart of *The invisible painting*. Gabriel is referring here to his mother's wartime mistreatment by neighbours in the south of France after her lover, the German Surrealist Max Ernst, was incarcerated as an enemy alien. Yet it is a statement that applies to the forces and institutions of normalisation more broadly. Normality, that is, describes a condition of emotional and spiritual impoverishment that fuels and reproduces cruelty, social division, militarism, racism. 'How easy it is to reimagine other people's difference as an offence against the law.' Later in the memoir, Gabriel writes this line in reference to the deadly violence used to crush the student protest movement in Mexico City in the autumn of 1968, when the army opened fire on a student demonstration in Tlatelolco and, later, when police burst into a café and arrested Gabriel and his friends. The truth of Gabriel's observation resonates no less powerfully today, over half a century later. Even as I write this preface in the final days of May 2020, the United States is (once again) simmering with rage and unrest as protests against the police murder of (yet another) unarmed Black man, George Floyd, have faced repression by militarised police forces and white supremacist government rhetoric. How easy it is to reimagine other people's difference as an offence against the law.

The invisible painting tells the story of an artist – and a family – dedicated to resisting emotional impoverishment and the catastrophe it reproduces in the world. Arriving in Mexico City in 1942 as a war refugee, the British-born writer and artist Leonora Carrington (1917–2011) married the Hungarian photographer Emérico 'Chiki' Weisz (1911–2007), a refugee and Holocaust survivor. Gabriel's childhood unfolded during a period of mourning and reconstruction, when Leonora and her circle of friends – including Surrealist poets and artists such as Remedios Varo, Benjamin Péret, Katy Horna, Octavio Paz, Alice Rahon, and Juan Soriano – forged a new, surrogate family. And no less importantly: Gabriel came of age during a period in which they persisted in their artistic and intellectual experimentation. To resist emotional impoverishment requires a fundamental shift in the way people use their imaginations. This means cultivating an openness and willingness to listen, as Gabriel puts it, as well as a commitment to question one's own intellectual preferences. This, he notes, was one of Leonora Carrington's most admirable traits.

The invisible painting is a memoir of Leonora Carrington written by her son. It offers a testament to her imagination and openness as much as an intimate portrait of her creative life. Carrington appears here not only as a major international artist and author with a career spanning two continents and eight decades, but also as a mother, a friend, a teacher, and a storyteller. Born in Lancashire, England, in 1917, Leonora Carrington studied art with Amédée Ozenfant in London before joining the Surrealists in Paris at the age of 19. With Max Ernst she moved to the village of St Martin d'Ardèche, north of Avignon, where she developed as a writer and painter before the Nazi occupation of France separated the couple. After she crossed the Pyrenees into Spain, the father of the grieving artist had her committed to a Spanish asylum in Santander. Carrington recounts this terrifying experience in her wartime memoir *Down Below*. Gabriel retells the story of his mother's subsequent escape and voyage to New York, where she collaborated with André Breton and other Surrealist refugees before arriving in Mexico City. Carrington's literary and artistic career in Mexico has been increasingly well documented, as have her collaborations with other Mexican and Mexico-based artists, writers, and intellectuals from 1942 until her death in 2011. In Gabriel's memoir we read, too, about her travels abroad: her return visit to her childhood home in Lancashire, her reunions with Surrealist comrades in Paris, her impassioned visits to art museums and her several returns to New York. Though such visitations may too often play a minor part in an artist's biography, they loom large in the imagination of a child, and thus it is through Gabriel's eyes that we can witness the affective as well as intellectual life of Leonora Carrington as it played out in her family life.

The invisible painting is a memoir, but it is also a gift. Like the painting to which its title refers, the memoir traces out an impermanent image: it is an act of remembrance, an elegiac portrait that presents us with a vivid likeness of the author's mother. Yet unlike its invisible namesake, Gabriel's memoir is both visible and tangible. You hold it now in your hands. This is important. For whereas Leonora Carrington is no longer alive to speak to us, her writings and artworks remain to call our imaginations into action and to spur us to challenge our presumptions. Here, though, we have a portrait of the artist herself as she lived, spoke, took notes, smoked cigarettes, raised her family, responded to emergencies, and revisited the places where she had once lived.

At times, Gabriel slips into the second person, addressing his mother directly. *The invisible painting* aches towards her continued presence in the world. 'If only I could talk to Leonora now as I once could', he laments. At other times, his prose gestures inclusively to us as readers of the memoir, speaking to us as viewers of Leonora's paintings and readers of her stories. We, too, can become part of Leonora's surrogate family: this is the gift that *The invisible painting* presents to us. It is a gift that demands a certain responsibility from its recipients: a responsibility to participate in its challenges, to question our own criteria and habits of understanding, to live *with* and *for* the worlds it opens up within our own imaginations.

To this end I think it is important to clarify a position that Gabriel – and Leonora – have expressed with regard to the 'interpretation' of Carrington's artwork. 'It is fruitless', Gabriel writes, 'to search for meaning in these compositions: they are what they are, and that is enough.' This position echoes the artist's own refusal to capitulate to biographical or psychoanalytic justifications for her working practices or the 'deep meaning' of her symbolically charged work. This position is anything but anti-intellectual. Carrington's artworks demand participation; they 'beckon us to take part in their saga', as Gabriel puts it. This does not mean that the spectator – or the student, the scholar, the researcher, the devotee – is somehow barred from investigation. Quite the opposite: what Leonora Carrington resists are the kinds of extractive interpretations that *replace* the experience of delving with some kind of self-contained elucidation.

Carrington stands firmly against the commodification of knowledge. She did not live long enough to become familiar with the term 'mansplaining', but her writings are deeply attentive to the kind of toxic, masculine self-assurance that this neologism describes. One thinks of the scene in *The Hearing Trumpet* when Marian Leatherby conjures a white-flannel-clad, racquet-bearing dandy from her youth: 'Darling', the young man says, 'stop being philosophical, it doesn't suit you, it makes your nose red.'[1] The young man keeps talking but begins to fade, disappearing from view even as he continues to prescribe the reading habits suitable for young women. As a figure conjured through the memory of Carrington's nonagenarian protagonist, this tiresome mansplainer is ultimately subject to the conditions of the medium that have resurrected him: memory, fiction. For Carrington, to be philosophical is to take active part in the life of ideas; it demands a living commitment rather than a recourse to explanation. Knowledge, meaning, philosophy, art:

---

[1] Leonora Carrington, *The Hearing Trumpet* (Cambridge, MA: Exact Change, 1996), p. 21.

these words refer to a state of being and thus are irreducible to mere explanation – except through the repressive imposition of power. The extraction of meaning is, like theft or appropriation, an authoritarian act. Carrington's art instead encourages us 'to live simultaneously in two dimensions: to live not just our ordinary existence, but also in a visual marsh that pulls us in as we engage in creative imaging'. This marsh, like all marshes, is a place of decomposition and new life, a liminal site between worlds. At once estuary and breeding ground, it marks the meeting point of land and sea, of death, rot, fecundity, and rebirth. Let us not forget that Mexico City is built on the ancient lake Texcoco. A fundamentally unstable ground, trembling with earthquakes, it is bound up in historical as well as geological cycles of death and new life. This is the terrain of Leonora Carrington's imagination.

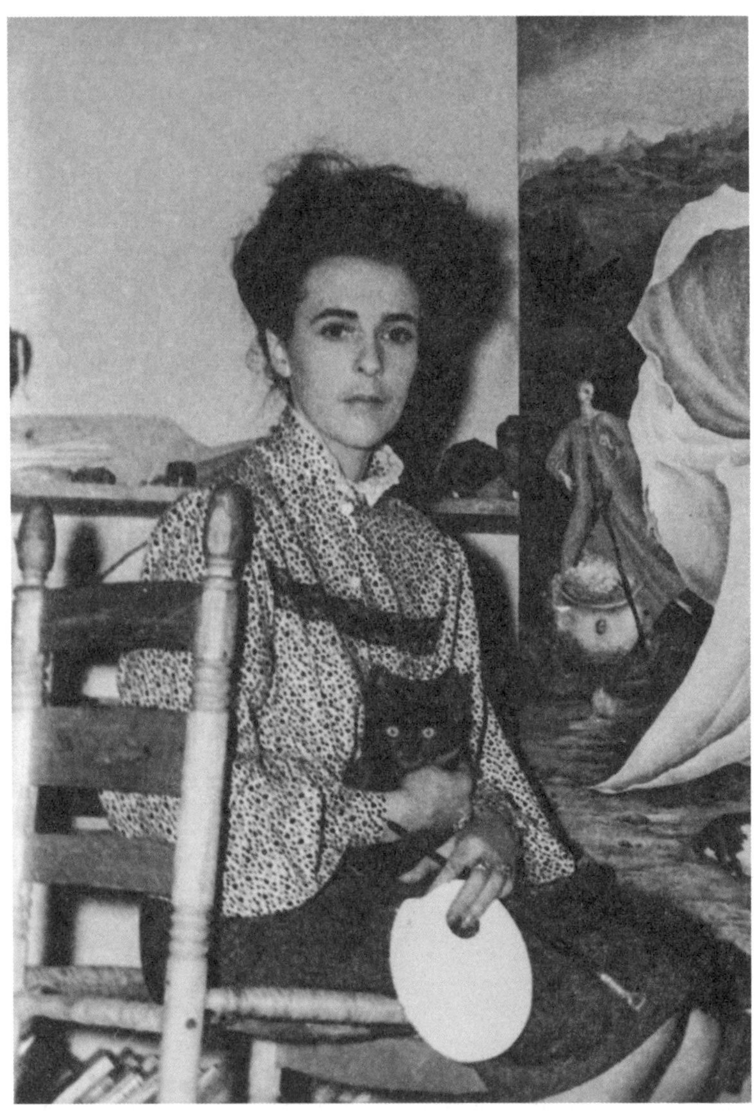

Leonora Carrington (with foxy cat), Mexico City, 1947.

The invisible painting

Life is so difficult that it is best not to give advice on how to live it.

My cats keep me company in the dining room – Mo for Morgan, the well-known English pirate, and Baku after Bakunin, the great nineteenth-century Russian anarchist. Two brothers with distinct personalities. My partner, Paty, blames me for the unruly behaviour of the anarchist cat, even though his libertarian temperament is undeniable. It's still early when I take a sip of coffee and set pen to paper for the first time.

To whom should I write? Who will listen?

My family is European. My Hungarian father was born in Budapest and my English mother in Clayton Green, Chorley, in Lancashire. Both were refugees from the Second World War, and, as survivors of terrible events who had begun their lives anew in strange lands, they lived with the perpetual memory of displacement. It was always hard for them to talk about the past; about all the friends and relatives they had left behind. We were a tight-knit group, but we were always looking to connect with people from Europe, that distant continent that now seemed unreal to us.[1]

---

[1] I want to clarify that the people I mention in this memoir belong to a chosen family; not all members will appear.

My Hungarian grandfather fell from his horse during the First World War, and as a result of the accident contracted tetanus and died. His family was Jewish, and most of them were subsequently murdered by the Nazis. Under the increasingly repressive rule of a fascist regime overseen by Horthy, the infamous regent of Hungary who ruled for more than twenty years, my father, in the face of dwindling opportunities and open hostility to Jewish people, decided to flee. He never went back to his place of birth.

My mother, Leonora, also abandoned her European – Anglo-Irish – kin, fed up as she was with a conventional lifestyle that did not allow her to pursue her vocation as an artist. I admire the courage she must have had to leave behind a father who never understood her, who interfered with her profession as a female artist. She moved to Paris, where she sought out the Surrealists and soon met Max Ernst, with whom she eventually moved to Ardèche in south-east France. The house where they lived gave them the freedom to explore their mutual creative visions. I have a photo of it, in which you can see the external wall decorated with elongated *haut-relief* figures and the doors enlivened by horses my mother had painted (see Plate 1). Eventually, though, all the visual poetry the pair of them invested in that place was destroyed by war. Max, deemed an 'undesirable foreigner' by the French authorities, was imprisoned at Camp des Milles, leaving behind a shattered Leonora to struggle under the weight of her own desperation. The town where they had spent blissful times together became for her a kind of hell, hostile and unwelcoming. She barely ate, overcome with grief as she was. The locals, who both hated and envied the life she led with Max, turned their backs on her, refusing to help. To those who live in emotional poverty, other people's happiness can be perceived as a threat. As a lonely, wounded woman, Leonora was an easy target.

My father, who went by the nickname Chiki, was still a young man when he left Hungary accompanied by his friend Robert Capa,

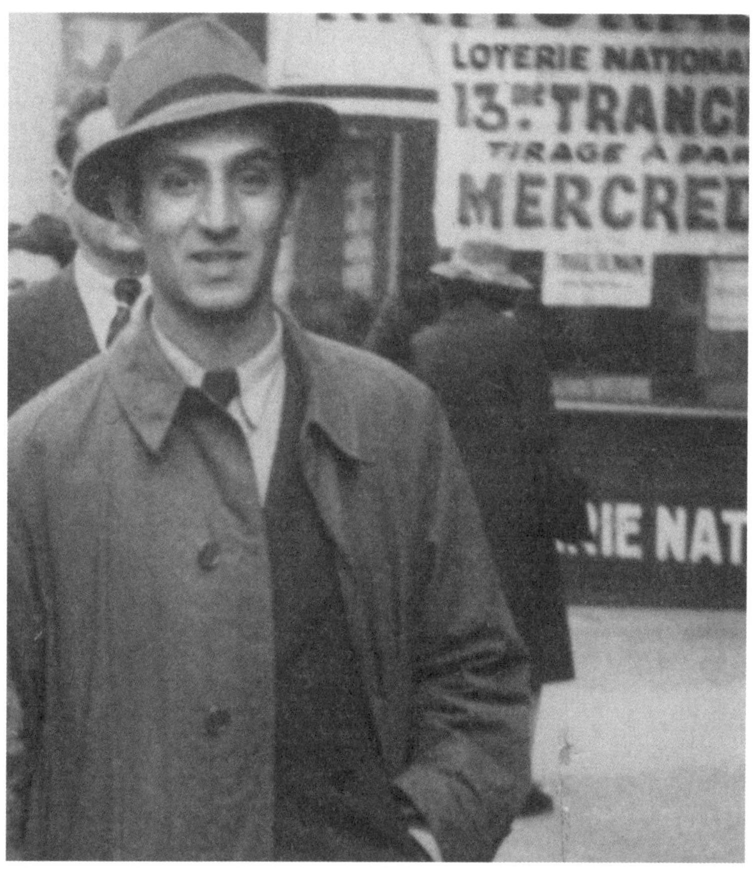

Emerico Weisz, *Chiki*, Paris.

with whom he worked as a war photographer during the Spanish Civil War. In later life my father kept to himself, revealing little about the unspeakable crimes his family had endured in Budapest. The few details he did mention I remember with great clarity, such as when he described stumbling, during a stroll with his brother through a forest, upon the macabre spectacle of bodies dangling from tree branches. When Hungary was invaded by the Germans our Jewish family was living near the Gestapo headquarters, and it is likely that these unfortunate souls were denounced to the Gestapo by a neighbour. My father's sister and mother managed to pass for Christians and were spared, but his brothers were eventually taken prisoner and died during the infamous death marches, during which thousands of prisoners were humiliated and beaten to death by the Nazis.

War refugees of different nationalities have been making their way to Mexico for many years. Here, countless personal histories have intermingled and coincided. It was among them that my own life story took shape. When I was a child, we had a small group of friends who lived near us in Colonia Roma in Mexico City, an area that was once the preserve of intellectuals and artists. Katy and José Horna, both of whom were, like my father, caught up in the Spanish Civil War when fleeing a Europe besieged by violence, lived not far from us. During her time in Spain Katy became a renowned photographer, and her images are testimony to an era that ought never to be forgotten. For a period of time the Surrealist painter Remedios Varo also lived only a block away, with the Surrealist poet Benjamin Péret, in a pretty two-storey house reminiscent of Spain, France, or Italy. They formed a kind of extended family for us.

Several years later some fragments of these friends' narratives emerged when, on a trip to New York with Paty and Daniel, my youngest son, I visited the International Center of Photography. At the time there was an exhibition on the Spanish Civil War that included photos from negatives that my father had salvaged from Robert Capa's studio in Paris during the war. When German troops were already approaching France and an invasion seemed inevitable, the invaluable negatives were packed in a cardboard box, which was then taken by bicycle to Bordeaux, from where he needed to find a way to send it to Mexico. My father told me that he delivered the negatives to a Consul General in Marseilles – possibly Francisco Aguilar, who was the Mexican Consul during the Vichy government – in an adventure that later became known as 'The Mexican Suitcase' affair. Chiki himself was unable to leave France before being detained by French fascists, who sent him to a Moroccan concentration camp, but Aguilar kept the negatives for decades.[2]

In New York, Cynthia Young, the curator of the Spanish Civil War exhibition, handed me a DVD containing correspondence about my father's detention. One letter dated 5 February 1941 revealed the close relationship between Chiki and Capa. Another made clear that by 16 June 1941 Chiki had been captured; according to Capa, who had received no news from his friend, 'the revolting situation now unfolding in Vichy makes it imperative that we find him safe passage to Mexico immediately, otherwise we may never get him out'. The Vichy government was completely under the thumb of the Nazis: extremely conservative and openly hostile to Jewish people. Capa's brother Cornell eventually received news from the concentration camp that Chiki had been transferred to Oued-Zem in Morocco, where the Vichy regime sent supposedly dangerous or suspicious individuals. Eventually, and thanks to his friend Capa's interventions, Chiki was granted a transit visa to Mexico by the American consulate in Casablanca. He boarded a ship named *Serpa Pinto*, a Portuguese vessel that saved a great number of European refugees. In this same letter from Cornell, I learned that another visa was issued for Maurice Ochorn, a close friend of my father's. Maurice had been captured by Franco's regime and was having a gun held to his head every single morning. It's hard to imagine how these individuals endured their dire circumstances, or what kind of personality is necessary to be able to resist such pressures.

Another note addressed to Capa from Bodo Uhse, a German communist, writer and reporter who had chosen to live in Mexico since 1940, traced Chiki's movements once he arrived in Mexico:

---

[2] See Cynthia Young (ed.), *The Mexican Suitcase: Spanish Civil War Negatives of Capa, Chim and Taro*, International Centre of Photography (New York: Steidel, 2010), p. 7. I also consulted letters on a DVD that was given to me by Cynthia Young and which I mention in the following paragraphs.

I saw your friend Emeric – he was carrying a small suitcase when he arrived and had the saddest look in his eyes. Some Jewish friends took care of him. I tried to invite him to my place so we could talk, but he called me back to ask if we could meet at Café Ritz. When I asked him when, he assured me he was there almost all the time.

My father talked about his time in the Moroccan concentration camp only rarely, but he once mentioned that when he woke one morning, he narrowly avoided stepping on a huge black scorpion. This image became engraved in my mind, a symbol of those terrible days in which he endured unbearable temperatures, abuse, humiliation and hunger. I met a Moroccan intellectual in Paris once, and when I dared mention Chiki's plight he flatly denied that any concentration camps had existed in Morocco. This is relatively common among countries that collaborated with the Nazis – they cover their historical aberrations with a veil of innocence. It falls to the victims themselves to denounce them and provide the facts. Capa, at least, with his mention of the 'revolting situation in Vichy', understood what Chiki had endured.

Leonora's experience of the war was equally gruelling. Roland Penrose, an artist and collector, sent a letter making clear his willingness to help her after Max Ernst was imprisoned as an 'enemy alien' on account of his German nationality.[3] Max was, in fact, soon set free, following the intervention of Paul Éluard, a renowned poet and founding member of the Surrealist group. However, no sooner was he liberated than Max was arrested by the Gestapo, from whom he somehow managed to escape. Penrose made clear to Leonora that he was anxious to do anything he could to help: 'I can get together quite a lot of influential intellectuals with the help of Herbert Read and we could sign a letter together', he wrote. Read, who was a poet and historian as well as an expert on

---

[3] Roland Penrose's letter belongs to my personal archive.

Surrealism, organised, along with Penrose and David Gascoyne, the first International Surrealist Exhibition in London in 1936. In fact, Leonora was introduced to this new style via Read's book *Surrealism*, which had been a gift from her mother. Penrose's letter ends with an update on how life was for him and his partner (later wife), the war photographer and Surrealist artist Lee Miller:

> We have been here from the start. Lee is staying rather than escaping to the USA. As you can imagine that makes all the difference to me; I am working privately in camouflage and Lee is taking courses in First Aid. London is all blacked out and what amusement we get is very limited. It's all in the dark. How unlike all we have known and enjoyed together. Give my love to Max when you see him. This nightmare can't go on forever.
> With no end of love to you
> Roland
> Lee

These lines offer a personal response to the dreadful situation Max and Leonora were enduring, while revealing the atmosphere of fear and destruction prevalent during the Blitz, that relentless German bombing offensive against Britain in 1940 and 1941. Although Roland affirms that 'this nightmare can't go on forever', it was enough to destroy Leonora's relationship with Max, and it changed Leonora drastically.

All these events bring to mind my experience with my grandmother. I met my maternal grandmother, Maureen Moorhead, on two different occasions: once when I was a child and she still lived in Hazelwood, and a second time during my adolescence, when she lived in a flat in London. She had chosen this relatively small home for her old age, as it had become increasingly difficult to maintain the grandiose style of accommodation she had enjoyed before the war. During the awful period when Leonora was separated from Max, my grandmother tried to comfort her. Maureen

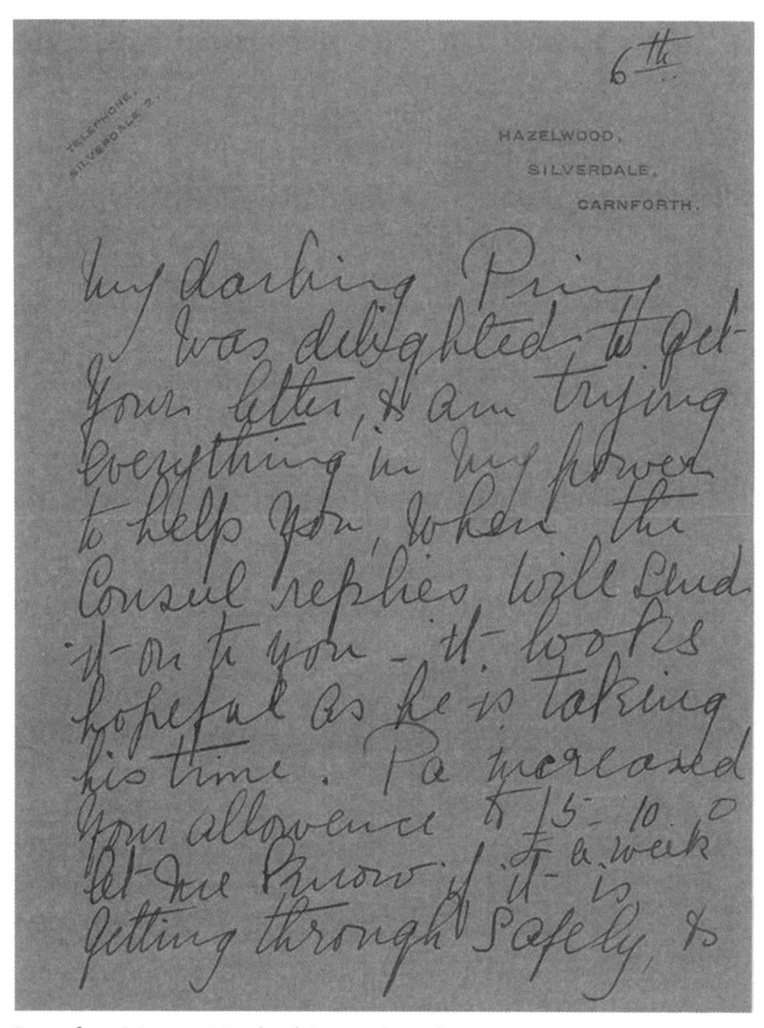

Letter from Maureen Moorhead, Leonora's mother, to Leonora.

was delighted whenever she received news from her daughter: 'I am having a cake made and will send it this week', she wrote. My grandmother also sent a hundred francs enclosed in an envelope to Ardèche. In another note, she wrote: 'I am trying everything in my power to help you, when the Consul replies will send it on to you – it looks hopeful as he is taking his time.' Later still, she expressed her concern by asking about daily comforts: 'Did you get a parcel of food from me before war was declared – a plum cake, sardines, stockings wool black & white you asked for?'[4]

I imagine Maureen in her house in Hazelwood. She casts about for some stationery, chooses a pen. The sheet of paper is grey and not very large. It is cold outside; through the window, she can see leaves moving softly. The war drags on. Her anguish is apparent in the note she writes, trying to persuade Leonora to come back to England: 'Would you go back to your own house if Joan was with you?', she asks, referring to a close friend of Leonora's. Everything is very quiet – then she adds, 'We all try to look happy and cheerful, but who is? Now let me know if there is anything, I can do for you, I'm not allowed to send picture papers, but I'll have another try, let me know if you can get them?'[5] Maureen understands how difficult things must be for Leonora. Nevertheless, the heavy atmosphere of war is impossible to hide:

Pat [my uncle] is suffering from an injured knee and is not very far away, he has to use a stick but is on active service, we see him once a week. Gerard [my other uncle] has joined up too. At times like these it is best to have plenty to do.

Maureen adds that she has not been able to see Arthur (my youngest uncle), who had just turned 14: 'Petrol is so scarce I cannot go and see him [Arthur]. All our love darling and don't forget – we will do everything in our power to help you. Your loving mother.'[6] Although it is obvious that Maureen was intensely worried about Leonora, I do not think she fully understood the extent to which her daughter suffered as a result of her separation

---

[4] This letter from my grandmother to my mother is dated only as the 6th, with no month stated, sent from Hazelwood, Silverdale, in Lancashire, and it belongs to my personal archive.
[5] Another letter from my grandmother, this one undated.
[6] Same letters from my grandmother.

from Max. Then again, who could possibly understand such a deep and personal pain? Emotions of that kind are inexpressible. Though it may have been Leonora's relatives who bore the brunt of the war in England, she was all the while living her own nightmare. The fascist atmosphere pervaded all. She and Max had, for a while, been able to keep the world at bay, in that house where the two of them found love and inspiration. But now familiar objects were painful reminders of Max's absence. The villagers were openly hostile.

When their relationship was at its peak, Max painted Leonora looking animated and joyful, the life pouring out of her (see Plate 2). In the painting she is emerging from lush, seemingly impenetrable vegetation, and she appears to move with ease. It's a scene that has always led me to ponder the enigma of both the painter and his subject. For decades we admired the piece of art – me and Paty, and our children, Pablo, Agatha, and Daniel. In it, Leonora inhabits a landscape that seems to belong to her; she is clad in moss, surrounded by a jungle of lianas. Years later, when Leonora was no longer with us, I was unexpectedly deprived of this painting. This situation belongs to a private part of my life; however, I not only want to record here the injury I suffered on losing a gift from my mother, but also to bid farewell to all the phantoms in that exceptional canvas, phantoms that nourished our lives, communicating their mystery to the room in which the painting hung. Before it was taken away, I used to scrutinise it, losing myself among the vines and exotic fruit depicted in colourful threads and jewels. Clad in moss, her loose hair flying in the wind, Leonora emerges from a glittering chaos, the green vegetation mutating into animals and fruit. She is seeking something, her pale, fearless face captured by Max's brush as she sets out on some unknown quest. Leonora was not always capable of finding this intangible something, and she would sometimes fall prey to anguish, discouragement, and restlessness, feeling the impossibility of inhabiting her own body. At other times her reward for this thirst for discovery was the paintings, sculptures, and other artistic narratives that emerged after a period of intense work, during which a lit cigarette was held perpetually between her fingers while pondering what to do next.

As I flick through Leonora's book *En bas* (*Down Below*), I find a quote from Jeanne Megnen. Leonora imagines herself wearing an imaginary mask that served as a powerful tool, allowing her to fend off conformism. Personally, I hold very dear this image of resistance against the imposition of social norms, because it fuelled my own struggle to become something other than what society expected of me.[7] In England, Leonora was brought up according to an oppressive set of social norms that regulated her behaviour. Finding Max for her meant liberation from those conventions. Her grief at being separated from him turned into physical illness: she was caught up in a kind of emetic ritual, vomiting continually, her body reacting violently to the pain of losing the person she loved. His disappearance was for her a brutal deracination, a violent disembowelling, and her stomach's unstoppable convulsions were a physical manifestation of her extreme grief. It was, at the same time, a cleansing ritual, a means of expelling the filth of human cruelty. The body becomes a stage where grief is tangible and enacted.

She describes, in *En bas*, her subsequent terrible experience in the Santander hospital in Spain, where her father Harold Carrington had her committed. As she revisited those dark moments in her book, she began a process of self-healing that would help her survive the psychological warfare she was now waging against herself and the medical staff who hounded her. Her testimony is very eloquent; this narrative happened many years after the actual events:

> Since I fortuitously met you [Mabille],[8] whom I consider the most clear-sighted of all, I began gathering a week ago the strings that

---

[7] Leonora Carrington, *En bas*, ed. Henri Parisot, Collection L'Age D'or (Paris: Fontaine, 1945), p. 7.

[8] A French doctor and writer close to Breton and the Surrealists and married to Jeanne Megnen.

will allow me to cross the initial border of knowledge. I must live through the experience all over again …[9]

From a stack of papers in my cupboard I pull out a very wrinkled document. It is an interview that Marina Warner did with my mother in 1987, when she still lived in New York. I imagine Leonora's Yorkie snoring in a corner, curled somewhere in her diminutive apartment. She had named him, somewhat humorously, Baskerville, or 'Baskers' for short, in tribute to Arthur Conan Doyle's *The Hound of the Baskervilles*, and the pup grew to occupy the role of both friend and guardian for her. In the interview, Leonora describes a series of traumatic events during her internment in Santander, under the care of a certain Dr Morales. This doctor pronounced her incurably insane and, via the British Consul in Madrid, sent regular updates to her father on the state of her health. They subjected Leonora to isolation and duress as described in *En bas*. Eventually a cousin of hers, Dr Guillermo Gil, who worked in the part of the hospital reserved for 'normal patients', paid her a visit. Dr Gil was related to the Bamfords, who comprised one side of my grandmother's family in Cheshire. Although Leonora was not allowed visitors, Dr Gil used his authority as a medical doctor to insist on seeing her: 'I had an interview with him', she writes, 'and he said: "I'd like you to have tea with me. They can't refuse." After which, he tells me that he will write to the ambassador in Madrid and get me out.'[10] They sent her to Madrid under the watchful eye of a guardian, Frau Asegurado. In a Spain ruled by Francisco Franco, it is easy to imagine the hospital environment as fascistic, with both Frau Asegurado and Dr Morales as so-called medical extensions of Franco's brutal, inflexible rule.

[9] Carrington, *En bas*, p. 7.

[10] Since I consulted this interview in a document from my archive, *Down Below* has been published in a new English edition, with an introduction by Marina Warner. Leonora mentions the detail I include above in her 'Postscript', p. 63.

Leonora writes about her journey from the hospital:

It was New Year's Eve; I remember it very well. It was extremely cold, and we got held up in Avila […] There was a long train with many trucks full of sheep, and they were crying from the cold. It was awful, the Spanish can be so terrible with animals.

I can see how Leonora applied her own bitter cold and desperation to those unfortunate animals. Her situation seemed to give her insight into the otherwise unknowable language of beasts. 'I will remember those suffering sheep to my dying day.' To make things worse, her only company was the nefarious, ever-present Frau Asegurado.

When they finally reached Madrid, Leonora marvelled at the size and sumptuousness of the hotel. The owner somehow managed to get round Frau Asegurado and invite Leonora to join him and his wife for dinner, alone. It was not the easiest of encounters; Leonora was aware of the fear she provoked in the couple; she was, after all, an inmate in a mental institution. Their wariness was evident: 'I could see she was hesitating to give me a knife and fork.' But Leonora was amused by all this silent drama. She remained a spectator, improvising an imaginary script in which the woman sized her up. 'She was absolutely petrified of me; they both were.' The wife refused to see her again, her presence proving far too alarming and menacing; an unwanted guest in the midst of polite Madrid society. The husband, for his part, seemed undeterred, and on a cold, windy night he summoned her to dine at an expensive restaurant.

It was here that Leonora learned that her family had resolved to send her to another mental institution, this time in South Africa, assuring her that the place was 'lovely'. A voice inside her head was shouting, 'I will not go to South Africa. I will not go to another sanatorium!' Meanwhile, her host, aware of her reluctance, sensed an opportunity and offered her an apartment all to herself. He moved closer, placing his hand on her thigh, promising to visit her there often. She was confronted, therefore, with a horrible choice: 'Either I was shipped to South Africa, or I was going to bed with this appalling man.' She found an excuse to go to the bathroom to think things over. As they were leaving the restaurant, 'there was a tremendous gust of wind and the restaurant's metal sign fell just in front of me, at my feet …' It was a close shave, and Leonora was badly shaken. Turning to him, she said: 'No. It's no.' He responded: 'It will be Portugal and then on to South Africa for you then.' Even when in such a vulnerable position, I am impressed by Leonora's refusal to be treated like a sexual object. This rebelliousness was always part of her nature, a kind of strength typical of her personality that later fuelled many of her artistic projects.

Leonora was put on the train to Lisbon, 'with my papers, whatever they were. I'd given them all away, but they seemed to turn up again.' She continued to recite her mantra – 'I will not go to South Africa. I will not go to another sanatorium.' Frau Asegurado had returned to Santander, leaving Leonora with a chance to escape at some point during the journey, but it seems that at this point she had fallen hostage to a fixed destiny, and she arrived without incident in Lisbon. She was met by a committee from Imperial Chemicals – one of the ubiquitous deferential envoys sent by her father, who was the company's principal shareholder. Leonora describes 'two men who looked like policemen and a very hard-faced woman'. Treating her like an infant, they announced that she was to be escorted to a 'lovely house in Estoril'.

There must have been a part of her that thought it pointless to fight such people, even as she continued to recite her mantra quietly to herself. But she had a plan – 'You have to think more quickly than your captors' – and so she pretended to comply with all their wishes. No sooner had she arrived at the house in Estoril than she began to complain of not having gloves. 'I haven't even a hat', she added. Thus, she persuaded them to go to Lisbon, only a couple of miles from Estoril. She pretended to suffer severe stomach cramps, necessitating a trip to a nearby café, and was relieved to find that the bathroom had two doors. She seized the opportunity to flee from her captors. With the money allotted to her for gloves and a hat, she flagged down a taxi and asked the driver to take her to the Mexican Embassy. After what seemed like an eternally long wait, she finally found herself face to face with Renato Leduc. Renato, an acquaintance of hers from Paris, knew Picasso and also had friends in the Surrealist group. He considered her situation before declaring resolutely: 'We're going to have to get married. I know it's awful for both of us, as we don't believe in this sort of thing, but ...'

Now that I know how Harold Carrington behaved towards Leonora, I can't help but wonder what strange reason led her to give me the same name as her father. A monument to masculine rigidity, he was bound always by convention. He alienated Leonora completely. Did he understand her at all or was he too intent on disciplining his daughter? His behaviour during that time meant that he was never to see her again. But these things are never simple, and her choice of name must have signified for her some sort of reconciliation with her father, although the last words Leonora heard from him were 'I forbid you to darken the threshold of this house with your presence again.' Perhaps she still remembered happier times, when they used to have dinner together at the Ritz Hotel in London. Nevertheless, Leonora recalled that during her time in Spain and Portugal she was 'as frightened of my own family as of the Germans'.[11] How could she forgive her father for his appalling behaviour?

It was not long after her escape that Leonora saw Max with Peggy Guggenheim. She noted the awkwardness of the encounter: 'It was a very weird thing, with everybody's children, and ex-husbands, and ex-wives', including Laurence Veil, a writer and friend of Duchamp and Man Ray, newly wedded to the American novelist Kay Boyle. Leonora notes that Peggy 'was a rather noble person, generous, and was never ever unpleasant. She offered to

---

[11] Carrington, *Down Below*, 'Postscript', p. 67.

pay for my airplane to New York, so I could go with them. But I didn't want that. I was with Renato and eventually, we went by boat to New York.' Still, she guessed what was going on between the pair: 'I felt there was something very wrong in Max's being with Peggy. I knew he didn't love Peggy …'[12]

Leonora married Renato in 1941 in Madrid. My son Daniel succeeded in locating a list of foreign passengers aboard the SS *Exeter*, proving that Renato and Leonora set sail in July 1941 from Lisbon to New York, where they stayed for a whole year. Daniel's expert help was instrumental in finding internet sources relevant to this journey. I wanted to piece together a few scraps of Leonora's life with Renato. Someone helped me find a letter she wrote to André Breton and his wife Jacqueline, and it taught me two things: how difficult Leonora found it to adapt to her new surroundings, and how much she yearned to talk to her friends in Paris. She admits, in the letter, that despite her love for Renato, she still felt isolated:

> I suffer from the pain of loneliness. I don't like anybody aside from Renato […] I don't want to go to the city because it provokes a lot of anguish. I caress tenderly my sadness and also offer my body as rich pasture for the insects. I have turned into a shy person, to the point of fearing the kitchen.[13]

Were the friends she left behind necessary for her to be able to believe in herself? 'I must be set free before deciding what to do, at this point I am only concerned with harvesting the mushrooms (probably) growing between my toes.' Her narrative swings between emotional crisis and humour – Leonora was always able to laugh at herself, and this ability provided an ongoing salve. She never indulged in her own misery.

As the years went by, she met my father, Chiki, and they decided to live together. When I was born, my grandmother made the long

---

[12] Ibid.
[13] Letter from personal archives.

LIST OR MANIFEST OF ALIEN PASSENGERS FOR THE UNITED

List 6

ALL ALIENS arriving at a port of continental United States from a foreign port or a port of the insular possessions of the United States, and all aliens arriving at a port of said insular possessions from a foreign port, a port of continental United...

S. S. _______ Passengers sailing from LISBON, PORTUGAL , JULY 11th , 19 41

Immigration document showing the departure of Leonora Carrington and Renato Leduc from Portugal in July 1941.

journey to Mexico. Bound by the stifling behavioural norms of English society, neither Leonora nor her mother ever spoke about the horrors that Leonora had endured in Spain and Portugal, or the fact that she never saw her father again. Those were the sorts of things that English people of that generation simply didn't discuss.

*

How am I to narrate this story of hers? I could pretend that, like the horses Leonora loved, I am simply following hoofprints that have hardened in the mud. These memoirs track down some conversations I had with Leonora, some documents and notes that I keep in my personal archive, in addition to stories she wrote that appeared in different publications. Paintings and sculpture provide different narrative starting points for this text, and the family album supplies another source.

I have vague memories of the mural she painted in the nursery when I was a child. Minute figures climbing a long, serpentine pass that rose all the way to the top of a mountain. There were some animals – horses, cat-like creatures, possibly a couple of camels – roaming about. It was a whole universe, one that was later whitewashed over. When it was, silence engulfed the room, and all the intimate conversations between the beasts and tiny characters ceased, drowned out by white paint.

I recall another moment of Leonora's creative work. When I turned 18 my mother made me a beautiful folding screen (see Plate 3). Shifting it one way and then another, I would lose myself in its images, entering into an almost hypnotic state. Its dogs would bark excitedly, having found a snake, or hearing the strange sounds of a ferret playing a piece only ferrets perceive. As I turned the screen, I'd find a magician holding up a simian figure like a shield, or a wild boar unconcerned with the momentous goings-on behind him. I would lie on my bed smoking God knows what. Leonora said to me, when she gave me the screen, 'It has a cold side and a fiery one, you can turn it around depending on the mood you happen to be in.' My mother was an accomplished gardener, and when someone gave her some marijuana seeds, she sowed them on the roof, where they got plenty of sunshine. They thrived, growing exuberantly. She allotted a section of the wardrobe to drying out the plants, and our modest crop exuded a deep perfume that made your head spin. Before long it was ready to share with all our friends and acquaintances, who began to show up with some excuse or other, or sometimes with no excuse at all. We rolled joints. Katy Horna had at some point given me a whole cigarette-rolling set, and now I could finally put the device to proper use. We'd smoke and chat. At some point, one of my girlfriends shared the secret art of baking hash brownies, though they didn't turn out quite how we'd hoped. After enduring some acute intestinal discomfort, we abandoned the enterprise in favour of the more traditional method of inhaling.

*

I find that memory jumps like an overactive cat, so now I return to my infancy. One afternoon, when I was about five years old, Leonora and I walked down Avenida Álvaro Obregón on our way to Remedios Varo's small but inviting flat. While she and my mother gossiped and smoked, laughing intermittently, I made friends with her lovely grey cats, who would leap out and then vanish, flashing their soft tails. One moment they'd tread cautiously with their velvety paws, the next slide at top speed over the wooden floorboards, spurred on by infinite curiosity. They each had an enigmatic personality that I gradually got to know: the wise one would find himself a spot up high where he'd settle in for a long meditation; the crafty one would whisper secrets to the coquettish one, who kept her disdainful distance. They all had something to say.

In that flat, in a transparent bell jar above one of the living room cupboards, stood a remarkable skeleton, a creature assembled out of an assortment of chicken bones, which Remedios had carefully laid out in the sun to dry. This was none other than the celebrated *Homo rodans* (1959), a wheeled predecessor to *Homo sapiens*, as she explained in an invented palaeontological treatise that accompanied the piece. It's easy to see why this fragile, bone-white object was so captivating. A kind of visual toy, it makes the viewer wonder how many sweltering hot deserts it traversed, how many jungles it cycled through in days gone by. It looked very lightweight, almost like an avian specimen. Could it ride on the wind from one tree to another, or did it glide through deep emerald waters? According to Remedios's account, the *Homo rodans* was discovered 'in Libya,

Mesopotamia'.[14] Many years went by before I saw this inhabitant of my childhood again, when it was displayed as part of an exhibition of Remedios Varo's work in Mexico City.

Leonora herself also indulged in object-play; for instance, she once invited Edward James – a wealthy patron of the arts, a well-known Surrealist art collector and one of the first to buy some of the paintings my mother produced in Mexico – over for dinner. She served up, in the middle of the dining room table, a monstrous fish-creature with multiple chicken legs. On another occasion, she delivered a pig's head that she had found in the market to someone she did not like – except she attached the head to a misshapen body made of a garish dress and a pair of stockings stuffed with cotton wool. The figure was completely grotesque; a visual weapon designed to provoke terror and bewilderment.

At home, the kitchen played an important part in our lives. It was a communal centre where everyone pitched in, where Leonora taught me how to prepare and invent different dishes, including nostalgic delicacies such as chestnut cream or Christmas pudding, which we would always have on festive occasions. This was a place where we played games such as *cadavre exquis* or Exquisite Corpse (the player writes something or draws something and folds the paper, and the next person can only see the last word that the previous player wrote or the edges of what they drew). It feels strange to remember these scenes, which bring me both joy and sadness. It's like invoking a conversation with those who are no longer with us, whose voices can only whisper in our minds.

Perhaps I can revisit one such elusive moment in particular. It is my first day of school in Mexico, and a very chilly morning. I can feel Leonora's apprehension; there is an emotional current that runs between us. My throat is tight, and I can barely swallow. My father, wishing to get all of this over with, picks up his camera, a

---

[14] Remedios Varo, *Cartas, sueños y otros textos*, ed. Isabel Castells (Tlaxcala: Era, 1994), p. 93.

comforting object, and takes a picture of my face, a face that clearly demonstrates little enthusiasm for this initiation rite. Naturally, Leonora understands my terror. That panic at having to interact with boys and girls who were complete strangers. The stress of having to navigate a social world, of complying with all the codes of normal behaviour. Did that day remind of her of the convent school where her parents sent her, and how much she detested the place? Even if it did, she knew that there was always something to be learned from such experiences – places like that breed a sense of rebellion against discipline and conformity, against that toxic mixture of antiquated rules and religious prejudices that forms the basic structure of the educational system.

On one such 'normal' day, you arrived unexpectedly at my school and announced that we were to travel to Europe. My mother was scared of flying, so this was to be a long journey, Victorian style, boarding first a train and then an ocean liner. Plane journeys always feel unfinished to me. You never seem to actually arrive anywhere, because the experience of flying forecloses the reality of the trip. It all happens so quickly that you hardly have time to take in your arrival at a destination; your body seems left behind. Airports, on the sordid outskirts of cities, sacrifice character for an illusion of efficiency; saving time, intention seems to prevail above sensation. At railway stations, on the other hand, you can read faraway destinations in the faces of each person passing through, nomads ready to wander through mysterious places that fill them with anticipation, or perhaps with dread. With train travel, we expect the marvellous: a swerving progression from one region to the next, landscapes unravelling before our eyes until everything is charged with meaning. Eventually there's the exhilaration of arriving at a hallucinatory terminal, bustling with activity, right in the belly of the mythical metropolis. Here, each person is the keeper of a personal narrative that's woven into the atmosphere like some splendid embroidery.

As we set out on the train, we were not sure whether we would ever come back. Only a day ago she had had a row with my headmistress at Westminster School, a pompous English institution in Mexico City which never quite lived up to its own expectations. It boasted great sophistication, though it was never clear what exactly this was supposed to mean. The headmistress warned that I might have to repeat a school term, not that either my mother or I cared. The trip itself was to become the best kind of nomadic education, the trip of a lifetime. Leonora's eyes glittered as they always did when she was about to set off on an adventure. Her whole nature vibrated with excitement at this return to her always longed-for Europe. The sheer strength of her enthusiasm was magnetic, sweeping me away. When the packing had begun in earnest, she pulled out a sturdy trunk made of wood and aluminium, destined for her carving tools – she planned to get to work as soon as possible on our arrival. I recall that Leonora had two visions of herself: the first as a bag lady, laden with large packages and random objects, keeping up a nonsensical monologue as she walked the streets of New York; the second as part of a gypsy caravan, on a beautifully decorated wagon drawn by four strong horses. Leonora saw every journey as a way of seeking out that caravan. She'd imagine the scene aloud, dreamily voicing the subtle chiming of the bells on the horses. Moving along a dusty road.

In preparation for our trip to Europe, we had to visit a sinister building to get all the necessary jabs. But even the needles seemed unimportant compared with the excitement of being released from our daily routine – from the kind of ordinary Leonora most hated, where the senses are dulled by eternal drudgery. It was on train journeys of the kind we were about to take that I learned how to anticipate. This work of imagination is an essential part of any trip, full of promise and exciting potential, a land where no rules apply. Once on board, I began to grow restless as the hours dragged by and I realised the tedium of interminable wandering; I asked my mother: 'Are we ever going to get there?', and Leonora patiently responded: 'Learn to live these moments for what they are. Don't get ahead of yourself.' I had to be trained to live in the moment, to appreciate slowness and how to rest one's mind, how to be with oneself.

We were heading to our first major stop on the way to Europe. New York was our mystical destination, a distant and unfathomable place that my mother had dressed up in memories, some real, others more likely borrowed from some fabled landscape. In order to get there, we had to cross all of Mexico and make a stop in Saint Louis, Missouri. The past was left behind; the gypsy caravan pulled by strong horses was in full swing. On the train, Leonora was in her element. True to her nomadic nature, she sat comfortably, deep in her latest Agatha Christie – *Murder on the Orient Express*, perhaps, a railroad adventure between Turkey and France during which Poirot's mission is to solve a chilling crime. Her reading was interrupted by the dinner bell, always a welcome sound, and by elegant waiters taking our order. Outside, it was pitch black.

Over the course of the evening, our compartment changes its appearance, as a bed is pulled down from above and the train attendant uses a magic key to open what was to be my room. My bed there is like a tent, with a reading lamp and multiple pockets to keep my things in. Once I'm in it, I feel like I'm in a treehouse perched high in the branches. The train is a hypnotic machine, its wheels groaning monotonously as they race along the rails; it gently rocks me until I alight in the theatre of dreams, where the journey undergoes a phantasmagorical reinvention.

The next morning, we head to the dining car once more. We are jostled from side to side, and I have to learn how best to move along the corridor. As I sit by the window, the scenery changes continually. A waiter brings me an exotic elixir: American chocolate milk. Leonora tells me the story of her mother's long-ago visit to Mexico; somebody introduced her to an as-yet-unknown soft drink she called 'coki cola'. Each one of us, as we travel, experiences our version of the exotic.

Life with my mother was filled with unexpected excitements. It was imperative that routine be overturned, so our existence was continually acquiring different flavours and shapes. I was a character in a story, but I had no idea what was going to happen next, so I prepared for anything. When the train was finally about to pull into Grand Central Station in New York, an attendant advised us to start gathering our luggage and a surge of activity began. We had arrived. New York was finally real: skyscrapers that looked as though they were built to house giants, steam pouring out of sewers and subway vents as though an apocalyptic diorama had taken hold of the streets – except that instead of demons cavorting around, chasing each other, the streets were full of people walking purposefully, staring straight ahead, focused on their destinations. This was a place where you had to look busy. It was a cold morning when Leonora took me to the Metropolitan Museum. She led me to Gustave Moreau's *Oedipus and the Sphinx*, faced with which I tugged on her coat and asked, 'Why is the lady with the feathers so interested in that naked guy?' Leonora was always amused when she remembered this incident, and on later visits to see the painting would always remind me of my childish remark. Children seem to seize a sense of performance: why is this happening?

We were in New York only a couple of days before buying tickets to board the *Queen Elizabeth*, an ocean liner cruising to Southampton via Cherbourg. When I heard the ship's deep, beckoning cry for the first time, boisterously announcing its departure, my stomach flipped, responding powerfully to the vessel's voice. The liner was like a floating city. It had everything, including a swimming pool and a playroom where there was a sort of toy ship with a rudder, permanently occupied by an aggressive-looking child. Access to different territories was restricted according to social class; first-class passengers barely deigned to glance in our direction. I recall that when I was a toddler, I spotted one day a young woman wearing a rabbit fur jumper. I leapt towards her, crying 'conejo, conejo!' in Spanish, and accidentally grabbing one of her breasts in excitement. The lady was paralysed and threw me a look that said everything. Once my mother had detached me from the woman, she explained in a voice full of amused embarrassment that her son was a great lover of animals: 'Please excuse him', she said. 'He did not see you. Rather, he mistook you for a rabbit.' The woman accepted the apology though she still looked unconvinced and quickly walked away.

When the ship arrived in port, we disembarked and travelled to Hazelwood Hall, my grandmother's Victorian mansion in Silverdale, Lancashire, where we were to stay. The property's large gardens, which gave way to surrounding forest, promised a whole slew of adventures. While we were there Leonora and I took frequent walks. She would point to a pile of rocks and set off talking about the fabled community of elves and fairies that belonged to our family's Irish and Celtic history – creatures that would hide behind trees and take refuge in little burrows. The whole forest area seemed to me enchanted, and it remains a place I think of often. Frequent downpours would leave rainbow-coloured patches trickling down the roads, which my mother called 'witches' pee', giving the forest an even more magical atmosphere. Leonora adorned everything with her imagination, allowing the fantastical to triumph over reality. Her way of looking at the world allowed the forest to be transformed, for me, into an ancient, magical land. I wonder if this reminded her of the solitary games she herself used to play as a girl, inhabiting mythical places where she was undisturbed by the insipid demands of a charmless reality.

Our life in Mexico had always been self-contained; we were a small family. We would sit around the kitchen table, the dog and cat always snoozing nearby. Chiki would polish this table obsessively with linseed oil, leaving a pungent smell that lingered for a couple of days each time. I remember a bored guest once began absent-mindedly carving his name into the wood with a fork; Leonora stared at him intently until he registered her gaze. 'Are you accustomed to doing such things in your kitchen?' she asked. The fellow bit his lip, embarrassed and angry, but he ceased his mindless destruction. The time we spent in England was very different from our modest life on Calle Chihuahua in Mexico City. At Hazelwood Hall they exile children to the kitchen in order to prevent interruptions to the sacred and serious conversations between adults in the dining room. Although I was perturbed at being separated from Leonora at mealtimes, the kitchen itself was spectacular. Set against one wall was the famous Aga stove, imported to England around 1929 and a necessary presence in those otherwise chilly mansions. Food was laid out on a sturdy wooden table much larger than the one we owned back home. Leonora's former Irish nanny, Mary Cavanaugh, now became *my* nanny. She was always ready to tell a story about the Little People, the *Tuatha de Danann*, a pygmy tribe that inhabited forests, rivers, and fields. But the alluring and exotic English countryside, as I saw it at least, also had a cruel and sinister side to it. One day a cousin barged into the house in full hunting regalia, looking proud and confident. From his hunting jacket hung a series of bloodied rabbits, their elegant fur soiled. His shotgun hung down at his side, recuperating after having vomited all those

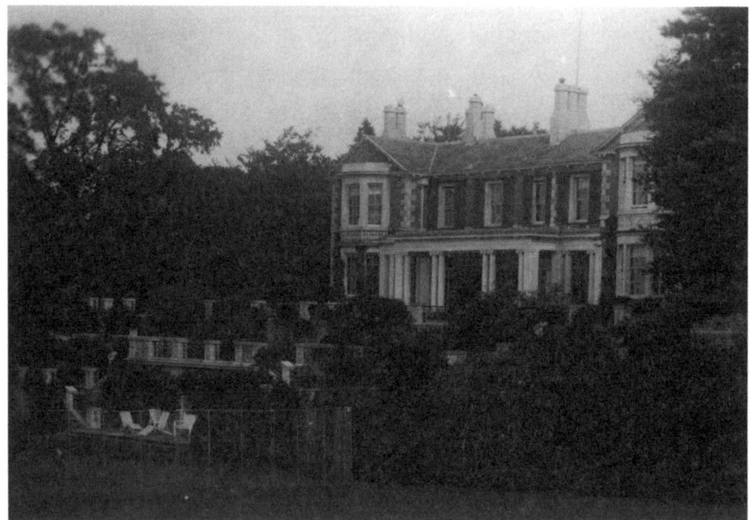

Hazelwood Hall, Silverdale, Lancashire, UK. A Victorian mansion where Leonora lived.

shots from its murderous maw. It is very easy, it turns out, to kill even such magnificent, innocent creatures.

Hazelwood was, at the time, a veritable museum of curiosities. The entrance was guarded by a suit of medieval armour which I fancied we would take back to Mexico with us. Not far inside the front door, on a table next to the window, stood a barograph in an oak case, displaying its fragile measuring instruments and the clockwork that turned the drum – another fascinating artefact that I both admired and longed to possess.

We hadn't been there long before my grandmother decided to baptise me. For some reason I got it into my head that this ceremony was a dangerous affair and burst into tears as it began to take place. She offered me some sugared violets in an attempt to soothe me, and as they dissolved in my mouth their intense flavour transported me to a land of pure sensation. They must have been difficult to come by, because at the time, just a few years after the war, sugar was still being rationed, as it would continue to be until 1953. In any case, thanks to the sugared violets I survived the dreaded baptism, and whenever I think about it, I can taste their extraordinary flavour all over again, bringing all my childhood memories and a 'crystallised' baptism.

Waking up one damp and chilly morning, I decided to explore the greenhouse, where my grandmother had told me she kept her plants to shield them from abrupt changes in temperature. I can still see it, if I close my eyes – that lovely Victorian glass structure. Next to the greenhouse tomatoes grew, unlike any I have tasted since; their delicate flavour was worlds apart from the insipid specimens found in America. I remain nostalgic for vegetables with real flavour. I wasn't long exploring before I came across the coal oven, part of the system that heated water for the radiators in each of the rooms. Each of these cast iron contraptions squealed like a haunted creature as the boiling water reached its veins. I remember, as I watched the gardener feed the oven with coal, a mischievous plan beginning to come together: why not lock him in, to provoke him, just a little? The temptation was too much; the scolding monumental.

The Hazelwood mansion remained the same rigid, severe environment it was for Leonora as a child, before she was sent to the nuns; a time she remembered with mixed feelings. Life's varied architectures come together in astonishing ways. During the years she spent in England, communication with her relatives, apart from my grandmother, was fairly limited. They were the family that never was. And Leonora, as one relative put it, 'was the black sheep'. On my father's side, meanwhile, there was little more than a list of people exterminated by the Nazis. In Hungary his own father had died during the First World War, leaving his mother in such precarious circumstances that she was forced to send her son to an orphanage – a decision that had a lifelong impact on him. Unsurprisingly, perhaps, my father was known as a quiet and reserved individual.

In Mexico I pull out the family album one evening to cover some aspects of Leonora's life in England and out pops Leonora as a teenager. There is a question mark written underneath the photo. Did she mean to mark uncertainty about the photo's origin, or was she simply struck by the weirdness of her own previous demeanour, as we all are when seeing a version of ourselves that is otherwise lost to the passage of time? I turn the page and see Crookhey Hall, where she spent a number of years as a child. The house brings back the time when, only a few years ago while staying in Liverpool, my son Danny and I were taken to Crookhey Hall. The Victorian mansion, which an acquaintance referred to as 'lavatory gothic', surged up like a revenant in some of Leonora's paintings, surrounded by spectral entities flying or levitating across the countryside (see Plate 4). As I look at the house, I think she will always haunt this place of her infancy, via the creatures she painted out of the stuff of a vanishing past. Are you here now, Leonora? Danny and I keep silent for a long while. Something vibrates between us; your presence, Leonora, is immured in this place. You, who when

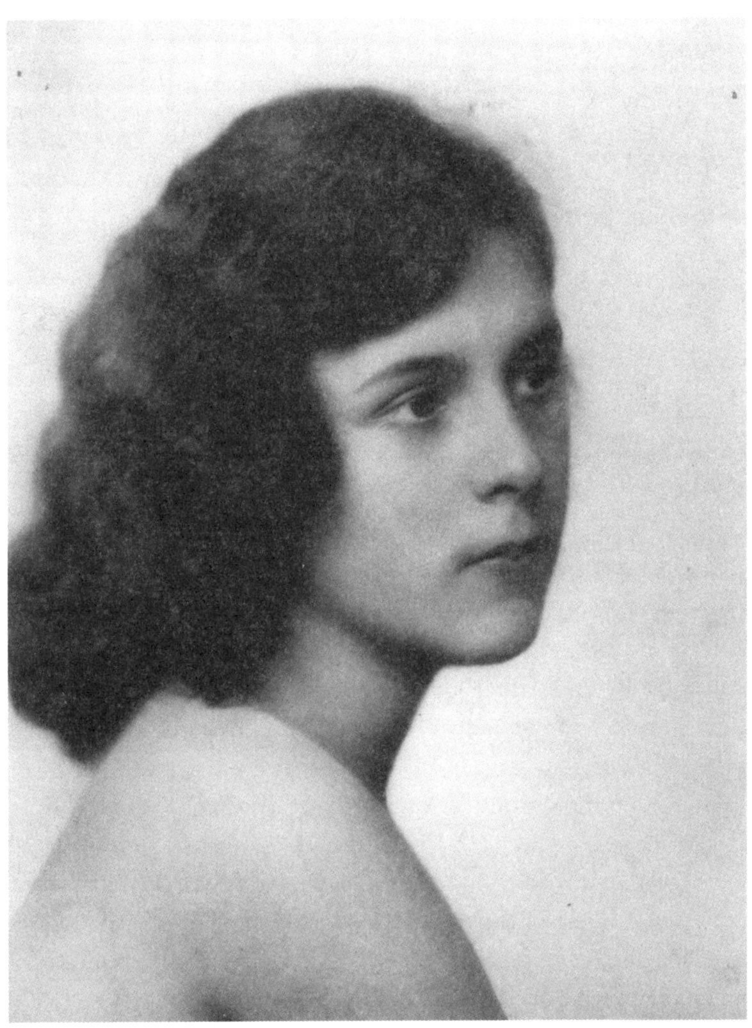

Leonora Carrington.

you were a child believed the place to be haunted by Colonel Bird, the man who built the mansion for himself.

At my house in Mexico, I turn the page again and find her as a child surrounded by toy animals. She always had a special connection with animals, as is evident from the bestiary that inhabits her collected works – a pictorial menagerie. And here is another

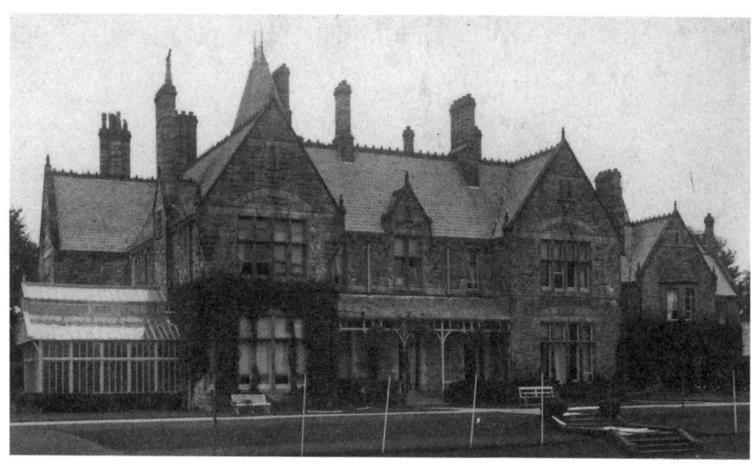

Crookhey Hall, Cockerham, UK. The house where Leonora was born.

snapshot of her as a child, taken at a costume party. Pat, the eldest, is sitting dressed as a white clown; Gerard wears what seems to be hunting attire; Leonora wears a bonnet and long dress, smiling very prettily; and Arthur, the youngest, is holding a ball, wearing a stern look. I can identify a narrative through these images of my mother at different stages of her youth. There is a particular quality traceable through them, one that speaks of a life carved from imagination as a way of surviving in a world that wanted to shape her according to 'normality'. Suddenly I'm annoyed. Whatever happened to the rest of the photos? Visitors coming to see Leonora in Mexico must have pinched them, scavengers taking advantage of an elderly woman, waiting for the right moment to make a run for it with their booty. Leonora was always very trusting, so people could just take things from her house. Still, I was able to salvage what was left of this album.

The animals, which were, for Leonora, her guardians, take on diverse identities in her painting and writing. Imaginary creatures are brought to life on the page or the canvas, giving substance to her inner musings. I gaze at one such painting (see Plate 5). The composition comprises a clutch of horses, celestial mares waiting to

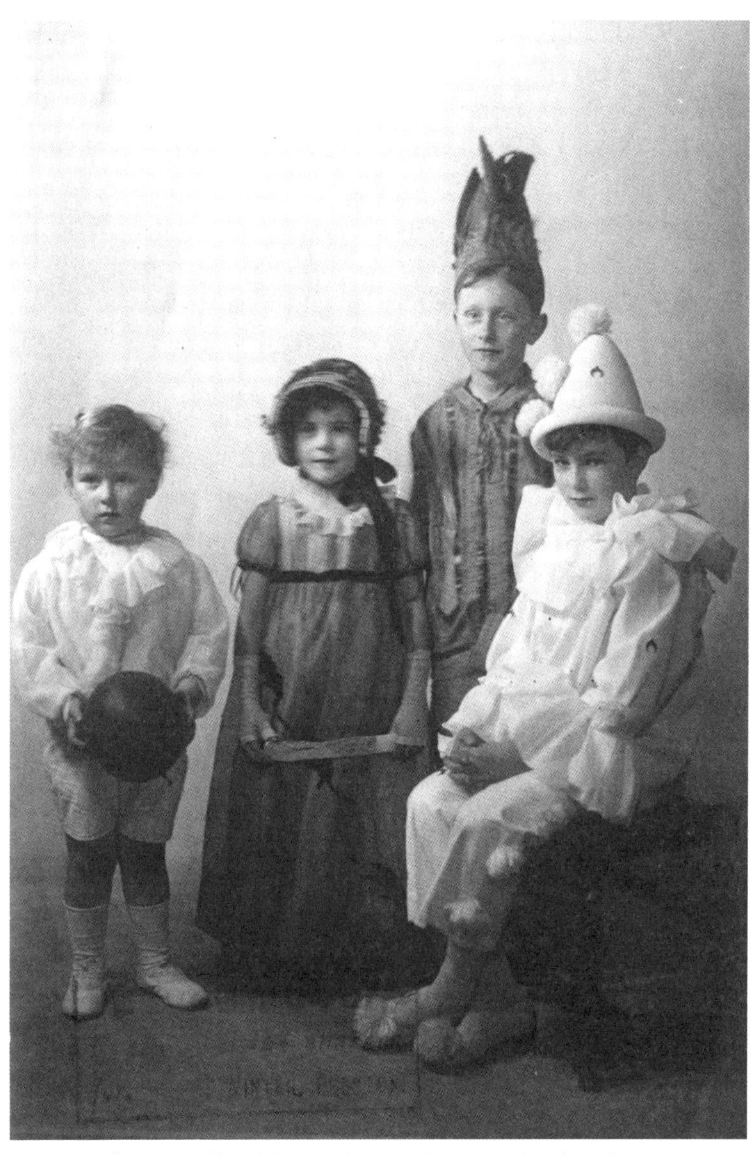

Leonora at five years old with her brothers, Arthur, Gerard and Pat (l to r), England, 1922.

be groomed in their stables, illuminated as they feed on a miniature sun meal offered by a Chinese figure. There are dog-like creatures, too, although they seem to be not *quite* canine, keenly observing the scene. Some time ago you remarked that these images emerged from your imagination, not from dreams, as many like to believe. For you there was a clear distinction, a setting apart of these different regions of image-making. Each painted being, spying on our domestic goings-on from their position mounted on the wall, has an intelligent look, seeming to know well how to guard their secrets and at the same time spark curiosity in their observers. It is fruitless to search for meaning in these compositions: they are what they are, and that is enough. They exist as embodiments of a legendary existence that can be glimpsed through the window of the canvas; they beckon us to take part in their saga. We are watchers experiencing a visual story. Leonora's is the kind of art that encourages us to live simultaneously in two dimensions: to live not just our ordinary existence, but also in a visual marsh that pulls us in as we engage in creative imaging (see Plate 6).

While working in her studio, Leonora never allowed casual onlookers. Any poorly thought-through remark might damage the fragile balance of a work in progress. Something shatters when an onlooker splashes their interpretation over an unfinished work, and so she kept her delicate skeleton paintings away from any prying eyes. She was right that critical pretentiousness can cleave apart the deep bond between an artist and their work. As such, there are special codes of behaviour that must be observed by anyone who is invited by an artist to view a painting. Leonora knew that there was something sensitive that should not be revealed during the process of gestation, so she always kept her work covered to avoid any indiscreet observers.

I look once again at the horse painting I have been describing. Each animal is like a hieroglyph written in Leonora's personal idiolect. It is up to the viewer to unravel every creature's story. As I later skim through some of her notes that I have in my archive in

Mexico, my attention is caught by the play she titled *Pénélope* (written in 1939 and published by Henri Parisot in 1946). It opens with the scene of a child playing with her toys. Among them is a wooden horse that comes to life; we learn that his name is Tartarus. I quote only a small fragment here.[15] Her writing stems from the secret domains of play and imagination.

PENELOPE: How beautiful it is outside. I can see them playing in the snow. What do you think they're playing – croquet?
TARTARUS: Don't look out of the window. In the past you were not so keen to look over there.

Leonora found inspiration for this play in her childhood nursery. By choosing it as the setting for her word-painting, she was able to dispel the loneliness she had felt in that place, where she would release her imaginary steeds. The character Tartarus is both a wooden toy and a living horse that communicates with the child, rolled into one.

PENELOPE: Beautiful Tartarus, run swiftly as far as you can. Tell me what you find on your way. Don't forget that I will always wait here for you … Always.[16]

Leonora explored at a full gallop on her dream horse, resorting to the itineracy of invention in lieu of an outside that she could not visit, confined as she was to her room. The horse in the play is the same imaginary talking animal from her infancy; she shaped for herself a subliminal space that most others could never know, because they lacked the means to represent it. Adults have largely

---

[15] I assume that the first version was written in French in Leonora's short story 'La Dame Ovale', where Tartar the horse is mentioned. Then came *Cheval Tartar*, a play. Then in 1946, *Pénélope* appeared in *Les Quatre vents*. Later on (in 1969), the play was published in *Cahiers Renaud-Barrault*.
[16] Manuscript from my personal archive.

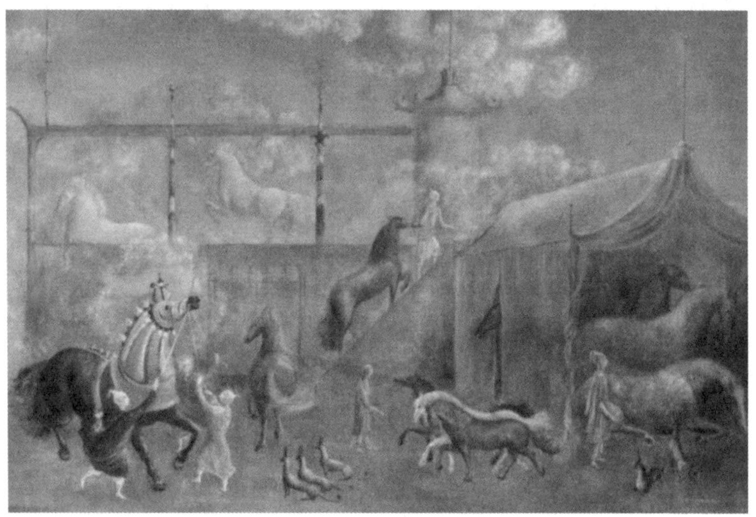

Detail of Leonora Carrington, *Habdalah Asejaledha*, 1959. Oil on canvas, 65.5 × 113 cm.

lost the ability to dwell so deep in their imagination because it has no use in the tedious reality they inhabit. Tartarus and other horses released the power of Leonora's subconscious narratives, inducing in her, and in any observer willing to undergo a mental transformation, a trance state. In order to become part of a character-substance found in the subconscious, you have to let go and conjure up the improbable from within yourself.

Leonora and I talked one evening, an idea beginning to emerge – one of those steeds that rides across our imaginary landscapes, shaping our dramatic narratives, as we shape Tartarus. Writing is a transformative game in which I become what I write, as well as what I have read. I get up and head to the library where I keep your books. I pick out a book from my library: *The Seventh Horse*, published by Dutton. The story's protagonist is Hevalino, a mare. Each time she opens her mouth something flies out: a moth-like creature. Another character, Philip, has fallen in love with Hevalino, despite being married to Mildred, who is pregnant. In his love, Philip's body seems to coalesce with the black mare, much like the way Penelope and Tartarus merge into one another. Eventually, Mildred is found dead in the stable. Leonora gives the plot an enigmatic ending: in the coffin, Mildred shows no sign of pregnancy, but there is a deformed fowl present, which nobody can explain.[17] In this tale, too, the marvellous-monstrous triumphs once again.

*

The warm weather caresses my skin. It is a glorious afternoon during the early 1950s in the south of France. I am no more than five years old and overcome with bliss – something intoxicating permeates my every fibre. It is my birthday, the fourteenth of July, and the whole village is decorated with flags. People are dancing in the streets, shouting and laughing, caught up in the festive mood. With great pride, I say to Leonora, 'All this to celebrate my birthday!' Amused, she responds, 'No darling, this isn't for your birthday, it's for the fourteenth of July. Today the French celebrate Bastille Day. You'll see the fireworks later.' I was somewhat discouraged by this news, although I did not completely believe her. In any case, I have remembered that day ever since.

Not long after, I stayed behind with a local family while you went to Paris to meet a group of Surrealists including Breton, who, along with a number of other writers, had introduced the concept of Surrealism in 1924 – although the term itself had been coined years earlier by Apollinaire. The poet Benjamin Péret was also there, as well as Mandiargues, a writer and close friend of Leonor Fini. You had long craved these meetings. The group felt so distant while you were in Mexico, and you had missed their soirées full of games and improvisations, where they threw around ideas, always open to creative play.

[17] See Leonora Carrington, 'The Seventh Horse', in *The Seventh Horse and Other Tales*, trans. Katherine Talbot and Anthony Kerrigan (New York: Dutton, 1988).

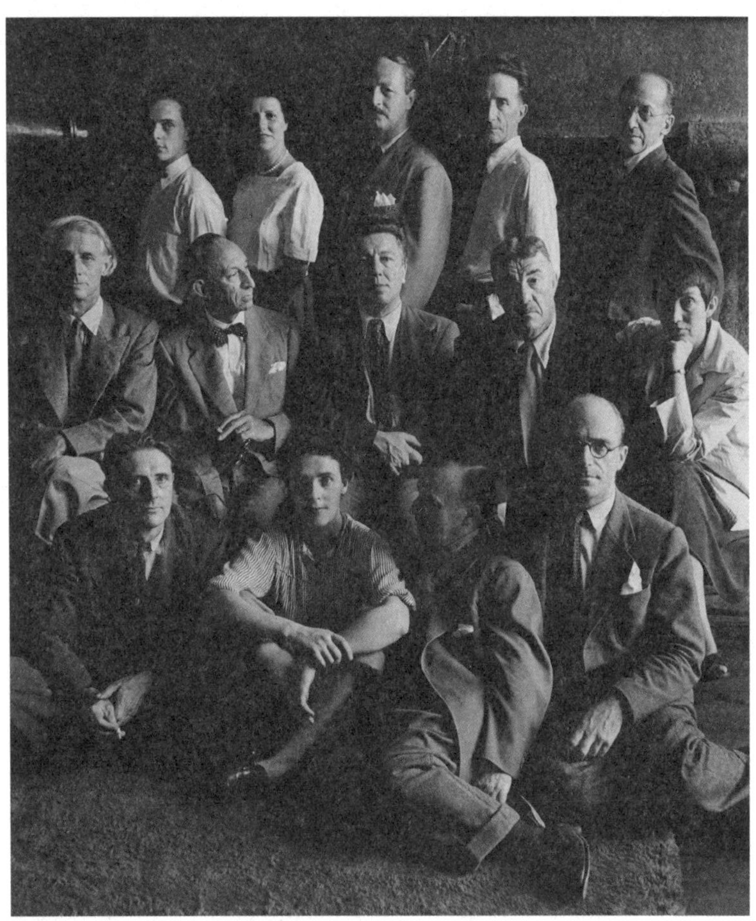

Artists in exile, New York, 1943. From L-R, front row: Stanley William Hayter, Leonora Carrington, Friedrich Kiesler, Kurt Seligmann; second row: Max Ernst, Amédée Ozenfant, André Breton, Fernand Léger, Berenice Abbot; third row: Jimmy Ernst, Peggy Guggenheim, John Ferren, Marcel Duchamp, Piet Mondrian.

Later you took me to the cinema in Paris, to see a Japanese film. I remember a pop-eyed character brandishing a sharp axe, lifting it over his head and embedding it in somebody's skull. The scene roused such dreadful nausea that you dragged me running to the toilet. In Paris we also saw the Argentinian Surrealist painter Leonor Fini, a tall, attractive woman permanently surrounded by Persian cats. She was delighted to see you again and decided to throw a party in your honour. I sat on the floor playing with the cats while you and the rest of the guests chatted. All of a sudden there was a luminous flare and an explosion of music; the cats ran for cover, and a dozen naked men stampeded into the room, all neighing loudly and bucking like angry horses, swinging their equine masks from side to side. I was spellbound, delighted with this celebration of the electric energy of horses. The scene was a lively little souvenir, for me; a celebration of weirdness and a perfect counterpoint to the fourteenth of July parties.

On another occasion I remember Leonor wanting to host a special lunch and asking me what I'd like to eat. I replied, without hesitation, 'escargots!' 'Fine', she told me, and led us to the market where we found a stand displaying a huge pile of snails, throbbing like a viscous creature. Leonor selected some and put them in a bag. We walked back to her place, and she went into the kitchen to cook. When I was eventually confronted with my plate of food, however, I suddenly lacked the courage to eat it. I was one of those monstrous children with very conventional eating habits. Thankfully, Leonor took no offence, and kindly prepared me a baguette with butter, cheese, and ham. Meanwhile, my mother enjoyed her escargots with a glass of Burgundy, of which I also partook, since in France children were allowed to drink a little wine as long as it was diluted with water and sugar.

At the time we were staying in a modest Parisian hotel and could not afford to eat in restaurants every day. I knew this, because Leonora never treated me like a baby; she addressed me like a thinking person and shared all her plans with me. Instead, we regularly headed to a nearby shop to buy groceries, which we would then conceal in our pockets to get them past the hotel doorman. These small acts of delinquency were thrilling to me. It was winter and the cold played to our advantage as the windowsill functioned like a natural refrigerator where we could store the cheese and butter, a trick my mother must have picked up in earlier years. These meals were all the more delicious for being forbidden.

I remember one grey day we decided to go to the circus, where a clown performed an astonishing stunt: with extraordinary deftness, he hauled his body up into a handstand, and then balanced on just a single finger. The small, covered tent gave the circus an intimacy and privacy that I have never come across since.

We wanted to prolong our stay in Europe, and when a friend of my mother's said we could stay at a house she owned in the French countryside we took her up on the offer. When we arrived Leonora opened the door, only to run out petrified screaming 'pipistrelle, pipistrelle!', 'bats, bats!', her Italian coming back to her in this moment of terror: in the early 1930s she had been sent to Florence by her family to attend her first art lessons at Mrs Penrose's Academy of Art. 'They really do look like flying rats', she remarked after calming down. We settled in eventually, and after a few days without anything better to do, I took it upon myself to dismantle a wine barrel I had found in the garden. The destruction was catastrophic. When she discovered the now-useless barrel, my mother asked, 'How am I going to put this together again? How am I supposed to explain to Sara what you've done?'

One morning Leonora woke feeling very ill. She asked me to go to the pharmacy for her, jotting down something on a piece of paper and giving me a couple of francs. I set off to fetch her the medicine. The chemist, who had thick glasses and a well-groomed little moustache, asked, 'How can I help you?' He had to repeat the question, partly because my French was far from perfect, partly because I was distracted by all the fascinating, multi-coloured bottles, and by the sheer strangeness of the place. A little dangling doorbell rang every time somebody came in. Eventually I handed over the slip of paper and the man went to fetch what my mother needed. As he put the medicine in a bag, he handed me a sweetie, which I popped in my mouth before heading back to the house.

It was snowy that winter, and the little insect-like white flakes fell on my face and head as I walked. The road was slippery, so I had to tread carefully. School was only a few minutes away from the house, but like most kids my age, I wore shorts every day; only once you'd turned 15 were you expected to wear long trousers. I did, however, have a long woollen cape to keep the snow and rain off. When I got to school each morning, I'd go to my classroom and hang up my cape, the snowflakes dissolving in the warmth from the lit stove at the entrance. Each student had their own wooden desk that opened up so you could keep your books and pencils inside. In the top right-hand corner was an inkwell, where you would dip your pen in order to write down the teacher's instructions. In this rural school, the teacher taught different age groups at the same time, addressing different rows of students according to their age and grade. This way, we were exposed to different levels of knowledge. When classes were over, I would walk back to the house where my mother would have a drink of hot water, wine, and sugar waiting for me. It always made me feel mildly dizzy, but the sensation was agreeable. Memory is often perfumed by such smells and tastes, which transport us into nostalgia. At the weekends, Leonora and I would wander through the French countryside, passing through an orchard every now and then. All I have to do is close my eyes and I can smell the apples fermenting on the ground. Sensory recollections charge those moments, and my sense of place remains built around them to this day.

A small window opens in this narrative to give an idea of an exchange between Leonora and one of her Surrealist friends. As I sorted through some papers in my archive recently, I unearthed a letter that Leonora wrote in Mexico to 'Zèbre' – Benjamin Péret, one of the major figures in the Surrealist group and someone I had always admired. In one of the many Surrealist magazines that I have in my library there is a photograph of Péret insulting a priest. The expression on the cleric's face is a real treat, a mixture of surprise and indignation that is unintentionally hilarious. In the letter, Zèbre asks Leonora to send him some biographical details about herself. She replies with the following, saying that she was a lover of precision: 'I established, recently, after many infernal conversations, that the information in my passport and on my birth certificate, that fatal pinkish-ham coloured document, was false.' Leonora then begins a series of humorous calculations:

> (999599999 (*) Ō Ō -9- Ō Ō 9), that is, two antelopes and a piece of wild bee honeycomb multiplied by a dozen minute chocolate monsters equals strange things, artificial insemination. Yes, dear Zèbre you must not despise me for my scientific genealogy. I was conceived by artificial insemination.

As this invented autobiography goes on, Leonora describes her mother as exhausted by a long walk and overwhelmed by sadness, full to the brim of chocolate truffles, oyster purée, pheasant, and other cold meats, which she eats continually as a way of filling the emptiness caused by her husband's lack of interest in her. She lies languidly over a special machine, my uncle Julep's latest invention, a sophisticated contraption charged with a hundred gallons of seminal secretions extracted from the male animals in his possession – not just magnificent Arabian stallions, but also royal pigs and fat cockerels, urchins, bats, and common ducks. Out of discretion I will refrain from relaying my mother's biochemical reactions.

In the letter, Leonora goes on to detail her own imagined birth, which was accompanied by explosions and vibrations that could be felt across the entire island, after which her family decided to educate her in a convent. The letter ends with the lines 'Dear Zèbre, I wish you a happy 1958, a year to be respected, seeing as we lack any other important recent events. Chiki, the children and I send you a big hug.'[18]

It is possible that such fantastical genealogies were closer to reality than the more official ones we are often required to write.

[18] Correspondence from personal archive.

How did Péret react to the letter, I wonder, caught up as he was in Surrealism's clichés of femininity: the sorceress, the femme-enfant, and the muse? Leonora never conformed to any of these passive tropes; she was far too wild to accept symbolic roles that others wished to impose on her. The femme-enfant is, after all, a narcissistic creation of the male gaze, in which women become mere objects for the 'inspired' male artist. How hard so many women have worked to shake off these projections, and yet still the game goes on. Leonora, having escaped her father's grip, was not about to fall under the bohemian spell of male artists and their demands.

France left a profound imprint on Leonora; she left behind what had come to feel like a real home and endured the suffering that comes with an addiction to place and experience. The return journey to Mexico seemed longer, somehow, although it took the same five days to cross the ocean. I have mentioned that on the ship was a playroom; this time it became a battleground, with certain dictatorial children imposing power wherever they could. These mini-tyrants of an imaginary ship were already familiar with the rules of how and when to command, and the room functioned as a tiny social laboratory of human behaviour.

The arrival in New York was always exciting, and this time in the early 1950s was no exception. We glimpsed the Statue of Liberty in the distance, draped in fog, her white cloud garments floating around her. It was during our short stay in the city that we were to have our first – and, as it turned out, last – encounter with my father's friend Robert Capa, the war photographer who covered the Spanish Civil War, the Chinese-Japanese War, the Second World War, and the First Indochina War, among other conflicts. Along with Henri Cartier-Bresson, David Seymour and a number of others, including my father, he set up Magnum Photos in Paris.[19]

---

[19] See John G. Morris, 'Preface', in Bernard Lebrun and Unidad Lefebvre, *Robert Capa: The Paris Years 1933–1954*, trans. Nicholas Elliot (New York: Abrams, 2012), p. 7.

It was a terrible day in 1954 when Chiki received a telegram in Mexico with the news of Capa's death while he was covering the conflict in Indochina, now Vietnam. This man's extraordinary life was cut short in an absurd way: as he was strolling along smoking a cigarette, he stepped on a land mine that killed him instantly. I remember my father just standing there holding the telegram, his hands trembling a little, his face unmoving. The news did not seem to affect him; he was the kind of person who had learned to hide his feelings. Some years later he developed a painful gastric ulcer, a physical symptom of the drowned emotions and strangulated grief clawing at his viscera.

But in New York Leonora and I were greeted with a cacophony of noises. There were porters everywhere with their red caps, offering to help us unload our luggage. I still find it difficult to understand how Leonora managed to be so patient throughout our wanderings, but the truth is I rarely saw her so happy as during those nomadic months. Back on the train, I rushed from one end to the other, gaping out of windows, peering in on people as they read newspapers or books in their compartments. A slow train journey is a sensory experience that gathers in the body. Outside, the landscape changes as though somebody is projecting a peculiar silent film on to the windows. Time seems to stop.

The journey over, we found ourselves back in Mexico. Chiki was waiting for us when we arrived, wearing his habitual Basque beret, ready to take us home. My mother had bought Katy and José's daughter Norah a toy chariot pulled by white horses, a replica of one used by Queen Elizabeth when she was a child. Naturally I fancied this present for myself, picturing how I would make it advance, hearing the hooves hit the pavement and everyone cheering as it went past.

When the holidays came round once again, I was thrilled to accompany Leonora to the zoo. There it was possible to hire a horse, and I was permitted to ride one without the help of a stable hand – I may have insisted that I was able to ride without assistance – who was normally required to lead children along on the animals. In any case, the horse bolted. I held on to the saddle as best I could, terrified, as monkeys, gorillas, elephants, and lions flashed by in a blur. People took cover as I screamed my way through, the horse galloping along madly. When, quite unexpectedly, it decided to stop, Leonora was the first to reach me. She was as white as a sheet, out of breath, asking if I was alright. I dismounted, trembling all over. The horse, meanwhile, seemed quite unconcerned after all its frenzied racing. Somebody very kindly offered me an ice cream. During our less tumultuous outings together, Leonora preferred to sit quietly reading a book, while I pedalled my way around in a red wooden aeroplane.

Animals were ever-present in our household. In fact, with hindsight, I can see that it was actually Guida, our legendary dog, who taught me how to walk. I used to hold on to the scruff of her neck as she slowly advanced, pulling me with her. If I were to believe in sainthood it would be because of Guida, who never bit a single person. It was a sad day when she contracted rabies and we were forced to put her down before having compulsory vaccinations in our stomachs the next day. Katy's husband José had us all sing a little ditty, 'jabs don't hurt, tralalalala', to make us feel better. After such an unpleasant afternoon we treated ourselves with a trip to a well-known ice cream parlour called 'La Bella Italia'.

One morning Chiki announced that he had a surprise for me. We walked down Avenida Álvaro Obregón towards a shop owned by Walter Gruen, Remedios Varo's husband. He mainly sold vinyl records and other trinkets, but the real object of my desire was in the window: a series of beautiful bicycles lined up like wild mechanical horses. I can still picture the one that was to be mine: a famous English Phillips bicycle in a glossy dark green. It was a sturdy object that withstood very rough treatment over the course of several years. It had a bell that emitted a gorgeously loud ring, a seat fitted with a little toolkit, and a pump for the tyres. Every weekend Chiki would drive to Maurice Ochorn's house on the other side of the city in Tlalpan, and I would follow him on the bike. One such weekend I had to stop at a red light while Chiki drove on, unaware. As I lost sight of the car, I began to panic. I tried to breathe deeply and pull myself together, to find some landmark I recognised. To my relief I spotted the American British Hospital, which was at the time located on Avenida Mariano Escobedo in Polanco. I left my bike nearby and went into a shop to ask if I could use the phone. This ability to become lost – for everything to be suddenly unrecognisable – in a city I supposedly knew was perhaps caused by my state of permanent mental nomadism, constantly moving from one place to another. Rather than keeping a close eye on my father's car, I had been distracted by other sights. 'Gaby, you've always got your head in the clouds', my father would frequently say to me. It is true that beyond the daily current of events I was always weaving stories. My world was constructed out of all the tales I read. The practical thing to do would have been to memorise the route, so I didn't have to rely on my father, but such solutions only ever come to mind after the fact. Eventually, Leonora came to get me in a taxi, and they put the bicycle in the boot and drove me home.

The bike was, for me, like my horse, a crucial character in many of the stories I read so delightedly about knights in full armour riding their trusty steeds. Parque México, whenever I cycled through it, became the stage for narratives I spun for myself along the way, weaving them around, for example, the imposing stone sculpture of a lady with enormous breasts in the middle of a fountain that rarely contained any water. At other times, I imagined what it would be like to live in an apartment or house overlooking that park. Leonora would have an ample workshop with a large window and plenty of light. As I gave free rein to my imagination, the park would change into Hazelwood, my grandmother's house in England, surrounded by trees, beautiful lakes and rare beasts roaming about. I'd dismount to buy some Dominican bananas, those miniature delicacies sold by an old lady who always set herself up in the same place. I'd sit on a bench to eat, my green mechanical horse waiting patiently at my side.

Yet the park had a dark side to it. Real life intruded in the shape of a pack of ferocious children who lived on Calle Parra, one of the neighbouring streets. This threat added an element of danger to my adventures, in which I would always overcome treacherous encounters with the help of my green, glittering horse. The park was also the scene of numerous amusing encounters. It had an artificial pond that was rarely clean, meaning that a thick blanket of lime-green algae that resembled a meadow covered the surface. On one occasion, a dachshund raced enthusiastically towards this 'meadow' only to find that the ground gave way, and she sank immediately into the water. Utterly humiliated, she swam back to solid ground where her owner, visibly upset and wearing so many jewels that she looked like a Christmas tree, rescued her. Leonora, meanwhile, would find a shady spot to read, as she always did, unconcerned by whatever was going on in her vicinity, so deeply was she immersed in the world of her novel.

This neighbourhood was also the location of many long conversations with my father about fiction, philosophy, experimental solutions, and problems, both personal and public, as we walked the dogs around the park. I remember when a dried-up pond was turned into a football pitch. People organised themselves into large teams and played despite the thick dust clouds they kicked up. I watched Chiki running to and fro with seemingly inexhaustible energy, screaming for the ball and sweating profusely.

I really don't know why, but I lived my childhood in a state of some anxiety, and this affected everything. I endured agonising homework sessions with Chiki, the two of us sitting around the table practising grammar or mathematics, both of which terrified me. I felt as though there was a wall around each school subject, so high that it was impossible to climb. After a while, Chiki would lose patience with me and start shouting. My mother would interrupt and entreat Chiki, in French, to calm down. Some of these exchanges were easily comprehensible to me – my time attending school in France meant that I could, at the very least, tell that I was the subject of the conversation.

I went through some tough times at school in Mexico. Antisemitic slurs were common, including from certain teachers. At break times, I preferred to sit with a book in a quiet spot, to immerse myself in that otherworldly domain to avoid being shoved around or having to suffer poisonous, bigoted remarks. I felt impotent, unable to communicate the atrocities my family had experienced during the war; memories one didn't ever want to summon because they were a reminder of death, humiliation, and mutilation, of relatives killed on death marches, or by an army of butchers, or by incomprehensible, intelligence-defying forms of racism. There were children who admired that herd of fanatical racists and a war machine fed by stupid discipline and violence. I often wanted to say something, but my retort would stick in my throat. How could I explain what my refugee family had gone through, the persecution they had withstood, to people whose lives were so far removed from such atrocities? People in Mexico admired the Germans with their 'perfect' discipline and, at the time, their murderous hatred of Jews. My family's narrative was a painful one, and each person found their way of dealing with its ongoing effects. My father, for instance, hid himself in his books. For Leonora, her art, writing, and other creative activities were her way of coping, and they all came together into an ongoing project of self-discovery.

For me, life in school was anything but contemplative. For several years I was subjected to the daily misery of fist fights. It would always start with a stupid, ominous phrase: 'I'll see you after school.' A mob of overexcited brats would escort the pair of rivals. First, a suitable fighting ring had to be found, out of sight of the school. The favoured spot was a sinister-looking place, with rubbish littered everywhere and a horrible stench from a pool of standing water. The sun often shone down on us ironically, charging the whole affair even further with its glare. The fight was over when the first person got a nosebleed. Anything could form a good excuse for a fight, including a casual shove or my responses to the bigotry that I refused to tolerate. There was such an epidemic of nose-bleeds from these brawls that it came to the attention of the head-mistress, who decided to purchase some boxing gloves for those still inclined to fight, such that they could do so without maiming their adversaries. Thinking about it now, it was not such a bad idea, as many people lost interest once much of the gruesomeness had disappeared from the endeavour. There was one English teacher, too, who made it his goal to eliminate the fighting. Everyone in my class had to write their name in a notebook. We walked to the dreaded fighting ground and swore solemnly not to fight any more, after which our teacher threw the notebook into the stagnant pool. Although the gesture had no shortage of dramatic flair, it did not mean that the fighting ceased.

I was involved in many such brawls; once I went home with a swollen eye, to Leonora's horror. Chiki, in contrast, made his way to the fridge nonchalantly, took out a steak and placed it over the injury, which had taken on a monstrous life of its own, quite independent from the rest of my face: a mask designed for a horror story. In the coming days, it underwent distinct chameleonic stages, from an interesting violet to greenish and brownish hues that only confirmed the alien nature of the creature on my face. My father was familiar with both emotional and physical pain, having himself experienced a tough childhood. One particularly horrific story still haunts me: his mother's drastic remedy for tonsillitis, which involved inserting a stick wrapped in a petrol-soaked cloth down his throat. This extreme procedure was undergone quite habitually, as an alternative to the surgical removal of the infected tonsils. It stands in stark contrast to my own experience of tonsil-litis, which, after a surgical intervention, involved consuming astro-nomical quantities of lemon ice cream. A certain Dr Maurice Hoffs was in charge of the operation; he had a moustache like Groucho Marx, and what he lacked in humour he made up for in efficiency.

This was, on reflection, a better quality for a paediatrician to possess.

Leonora was upset to hear about the fighting at school. She and my father had fled Europe as the Nazis invaded, and the antisemitic trend at my school was rekindling that old fear like a polluted ghost. The day after I came home with a black eye, she enrolled me in judo classes. Ironically, in the very first session, the teacher, who was exceptional, warned us that one should not use this martial art to hurt another person. Nevertheless, something unusual happened to my body as the classes went on: I obtained a certain confidence and inner strength.

Before long, I acquired a reputation among the teachers for being an incorrigible rebel. Leonora revealed to me that she had been expelled from school, and thus a kind of complicity developed between us. I kept being asked to leave the classroom and became intimately familiar with the headmistress's office, where long-drawn-out sermons were to be expected, sprinkled with various psychoanalytic interpretations of my behaviour. I was good for nothing and would end up a vagabond. 'Wipe that smile off your face' was a frequent refrain. I never responded, because whenever the headmistress mentioned vagabonds, I couldn't help but picture Charlie Chaplin twirling his legendary walking stick with undeniable elegance and poise as he walked. From the large, panopticon window in the office, I could see children horsing around as they laughed and played. This only made the place's atmosphere even more rarefied, more like a kind of altered reality. I felt as though I was trapped in a huge aquarium, suspended in water, listening to the din of screaming, laughter, and complaints outside the tank. Years later, a friend and I would bunk off school and spend the day in a nearby plant nursery where we would smoke, feeling like real grown-ups: deep, mature, and intelligent, with important ideas about sex and the world at large. We'd always head for the least-frequented corner, where young would-be bullfighters often trained. They shook their red capes while maintaining elegant poses, taunting a strange artefact, a bicycle-creature. For practice, they attached horns to the handlebars – Picasso would have been overcome with taurine jealousy had he been around to observe such an ingenious bull-bicycle contraption. The one pushing the bull-replica would periodically run at full speed towards the bullfighter, who would dodge it deftly, leaving a murderous look on the face of the one manoeuvring the bull-bicycle. Under such circumstances, it seems, we are unable to avoid becoming bullish.

School was so unpleasant that I ended up having a recurring nightmare for many years afterwards. In it, I was caught in a glass cell, forced to look at a glittering, infernal blackboard. Someone would knock at the door, and an emaciated, grim-looking teacher would enter wearing a severe black suit. He would announce that I had failed a subject I'd taken in my first year of grammar school and that I had to sit an exam. It didn't seem to matter, though I tried to explain that I was already enrolled at university. The teacher just shrugged, and said in an affected voice, 'We've analysed your file and the academic committee has made its decision. Our offices are open to complaints from four to six p.m. The toilets are straight down and on your left.' Without further ado, the fellow would turn his back on me like a proud crow, leaving me to contemplate the miserable future of my school life. It was pointless to discuss anything with this character. To distract me, every evening Chiki read darkly humorous stories, such as the one from *Struwwelpeter* in which Konrad, the protagonist, in the habit of sucking his thumb, flees from a jovial-looking tailor carrying a huge pair of scissors who tries to chop off his fingers. Or else the one about Max and Moritz, a pair of naughty children who steal a chicken by lowering a fishing line down a chimney.

One weekend, Chiki planned a visit to some Hungarian friends who lived in the nearby town of Texcoco. One of them was a ceramicist who made replicas of pre-Hispanic sculptures. These terracotta versions of hairless, pot-bellied dogs originated in the west of Mexico (Colima) in 300BC–300AD.[20] The ceramicist's wife was a fabulous cook and baked us some Dobosh torte, a Hungarian cake, and other delicacies, which we ate with chestnut cream. Yanni, their son, who was a bit older than me, showed me the kilns where his father and his staff fired the terracotta. The place reminded me of an archaeological site, with fragments of ceramic dogs and other figurines littering the ground.

One year we went on holiday with them to the beach in Manzanillo, land of the fat Colima dogs. It was a rare trip for us, and we stayed at the only hotel for miles around. Yanni had an insatiable appetite for calling attention to himself; everything he asked for he was given by his parents, although in return they forced the poor chap to practise the violin for hours on end. I was entranced, watching him play, the instrument resting on his shoulder, his muted agony as the bow moved, screeching, up and down the strings. We went fishing one day, and when I was the only one to catch anything, Yanni wept disconsolately. To my horror, the fishermen hauled my fish on to the boat and whacked its head with a club until it died. Needless to say, this was both my first and last fishing trip. At dinner time, the ten-kilo jackfish was set on the table, but I struggled to eat my portion. I preferred him swimming, free and majestic. One very sunny day we headed to the beach, and Yanni got into the sea wearing a full mask, fins, and a rubber ring. The sea lapped the beach like a giant feline creature, but the rip current was strong, and Yanni was pulled away from the shore without realising, so focused was he on the marine world visible through his mask. It wasn't long before he was alarmingly far away. Yanni's father realised the danger and leapt into the water, but he made slow progress, only able to do a backstroke. It was left to Chiki, then, to swim out with great difficulty and

---

[20] See Riley Winters's article 'A Dog Eat Dog World: The Canine Figurines of Mesoamerican Colima', https://www.ancient-origins.net/artifacts-other-artifacts/dog-eat-dog-world-canine-figurines-mesoamerican-colima-003417 (accessed 9 September 2020).

rescue the drowning Yanni. Back on the beach, the boy, gasping and coughing, immediately demanded to know where his mask was. 'I don't know', Chiki replied, 'I had to pull it off because you couldn't breathe.' 'You had no right', Yanni complained. Leonora, meanwhile, who was no enthusiast for the sun or the water, remained quietly in the shade, sketching.

Tehuixtla was a more frequent holiday destination for us. My father drove an old car that could barely make it along the motorway. Insects collided with the windscreen, leaving behind a sad collage of inanimate bodies. We'd walk out of the hotel and over a suspension bridge to explore the area – this part always scared me, because some of the wooden boards had rotted and you could see the river flowing below. Once safely on the other side, we'd visit the Borbollón, a natural reservoir where the cobalt blue, green, and turquoise waters bubbled with the steam emerging from underground. I loved dipping my face under, peering through the ghostly, ancient, underwater gloom.

The hotel we stayed in belonged to some Spanish refugees, but was also home, during the holidays, to two monstrous bullies. One year I climbed up to the highest diving board, where there was a cool breeze, so that I could sit and read. One of those awful creatures silently followed me up, and, grabbling me by my swimming trunks, flung me off into the water. He cackled like a character in a horror film. I had to lay my book out to dry in the sun. Later, this nightmarish pair gathered all the children together to form a captive audience, because one of them believed that he was poetically endowed. We had no choice but to sit by the pool while the so-called bard spewed out interminable love poems, complete with flocks of blue birds, girls with pearly lips, and eyes streaming beatific goodness. It was strange to see this stereotype of machismo caught up in such sugar-coated sentimentality. During the day, the pair of brutes played handball as a way of getting rid of their excess energy. Their father also took them hunting and ill-advisedly bought them a bow and arrow set as a Christmas present. With a dark look, the 'poet' advised his brother to 'run, rabbit, run!', at which point his brother sped off as fast as he could in an attempt to save his skin – not fast enough, it turned out, meaning that one of the arrows lodged itself in his leg. Off to a hospital he went, where he must have undergone a very painful extraction procedure. Having seen these more violent developments in their behaviour, I was reluctant to fall into the role of rabbit, fawn, or any other ill-fated animal. I sought for myself a secluded hideout where I could enjoy my Sherlock Holmes books, safe from predators. I immersed myself in the hypnotic Conan Doyle adventures and allowed all else to disappear. What a splendid conjuring trick reading can become!

Back in our daily routine in Mexico City, we would saunter on Avenida Álvaro Obregón to the Balmori cinema. I always had my dog Boni by my side, Guida's honey-coloured puppy, who had the same benevolence as his mother. While I watched the film, Boni would lie down next to the cinema attendants with Zen-like patience. A fountain decorated the entrance to the cinema, and at its centre was a hideous nude white statue, probably made from marble, lit up by a set of bulbs that threw an unpleasant greenish light over the figure. Despite its ugliness, this statue always represented, for me, the enigmatic allure of cinema. On my return, my father would ask about what I had seen, but I was seldom able to respond adequately – how could I explain that while watching the film, I had entered into another world entirely? I retained very little from my time in those darkened rooms, which I always treated as an opportunity to lose myself. My father wanted it to be a way of training my intellect, but I preferred this total flight into fiction.

In school, I insisted on my difference from the other children. When one girl accused me of not believing in Jesus, a teacher challenged me: 'Did you really say that?' 'I did', I replied. Her face was the picture of fury. She led me to the corner of the classroom and forbade me from sitting at my desk. I was to be made an

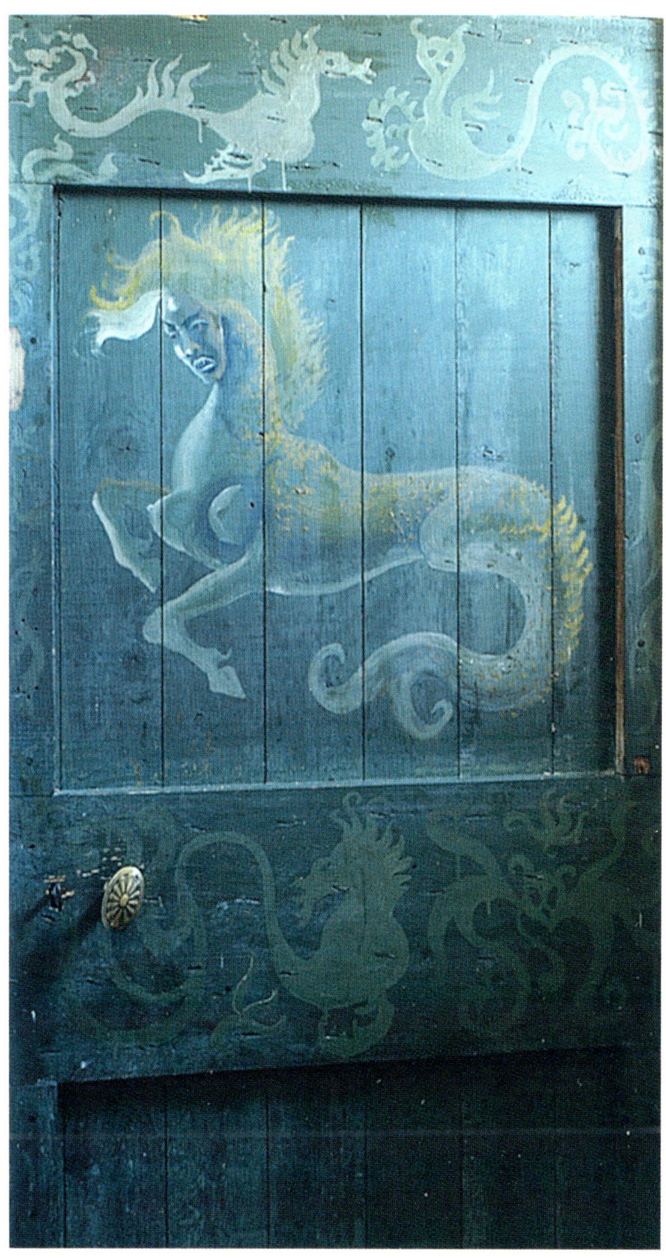

The wooden door painted by Leonora Carrington at the house where she lived with Max Ernst in St Martin d'Ardèche, France.

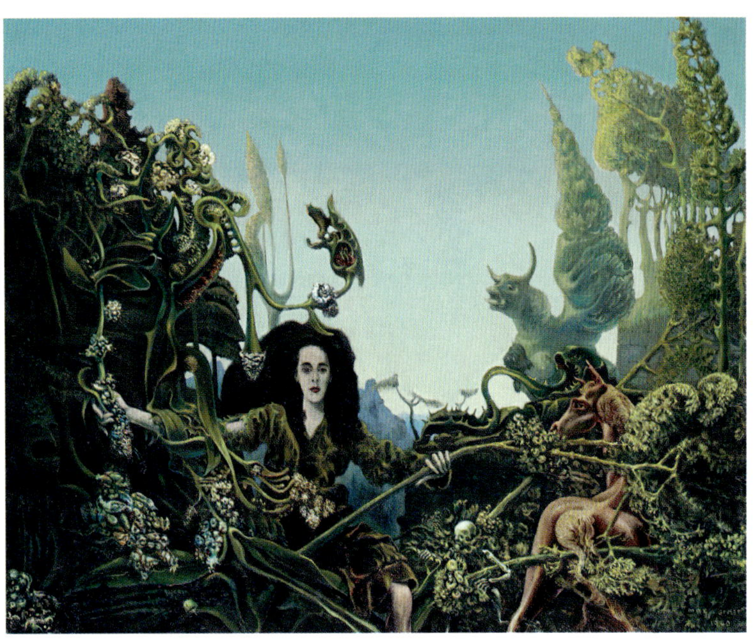

Max Ernst, *Leonora in the Morning Light*, 1940. Oil on canvas, 66 × 82 cm.

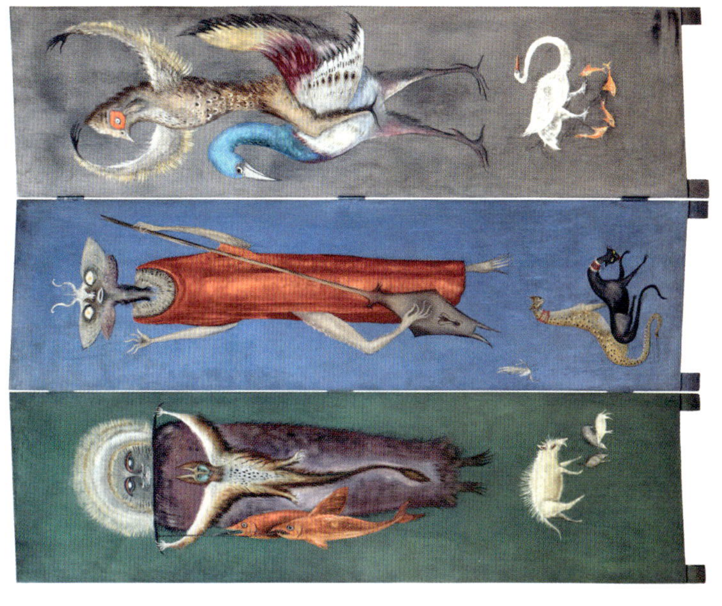

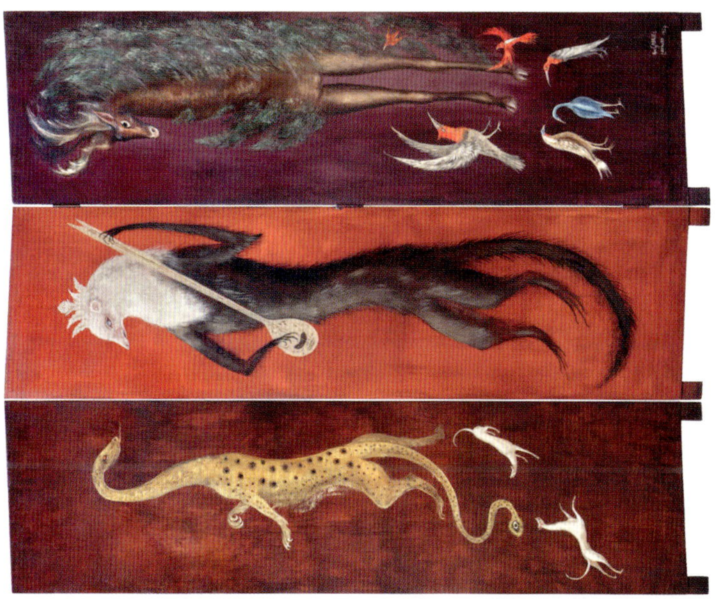

Leonora Carrington, screen, 1964. Oil on wood, 114 × 45 cm.

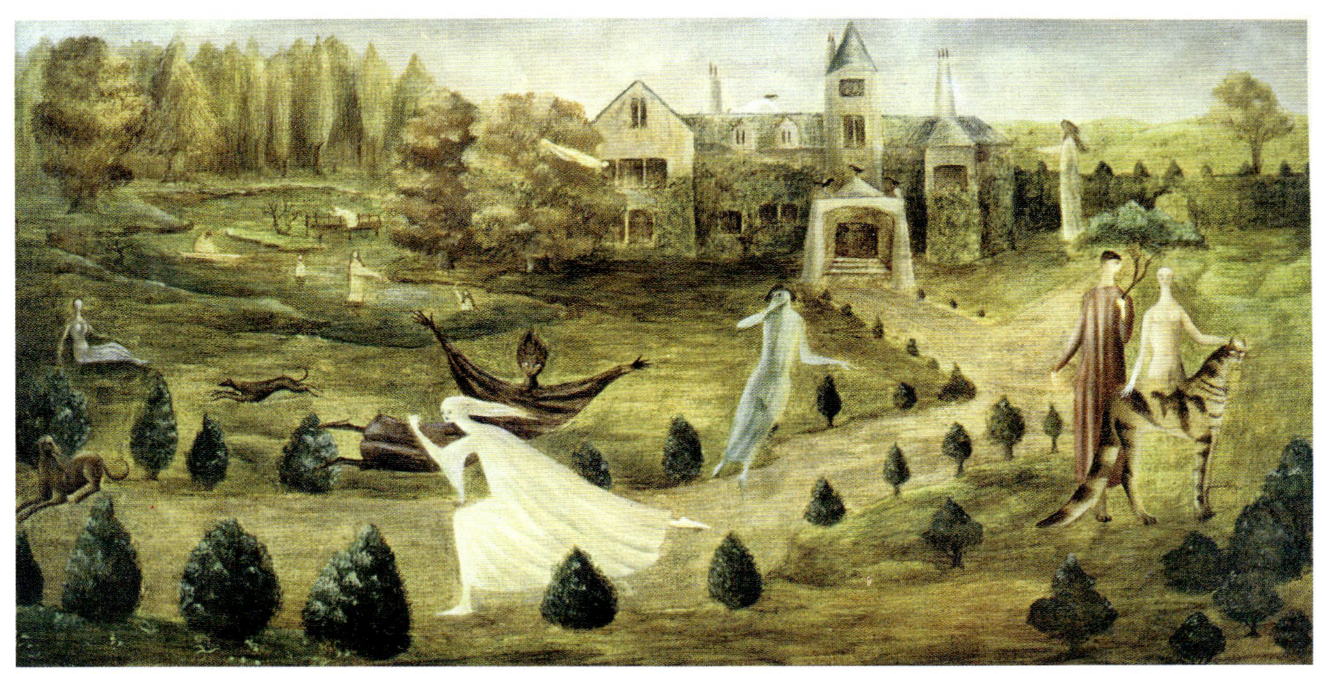

Leonora Carrington, *Crookhey Hall*, 1947. Casein on Masonite, 31 × 60 cm.

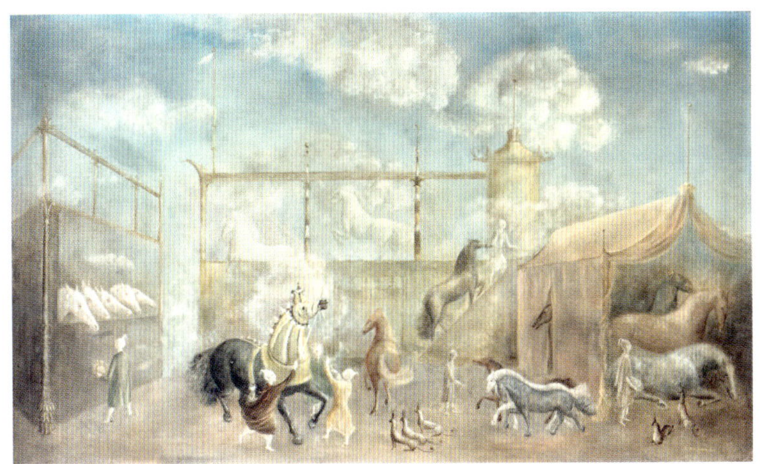

Leonora Carrington, *Habdalah Asejaledha*, 1959. Oil on canvas, 65.5 × 113 cm.

The thunderous galloping
from celestial steeds
were under the orders of the Lady of Storms.
A very special auspicious disposition of planets
for this day.

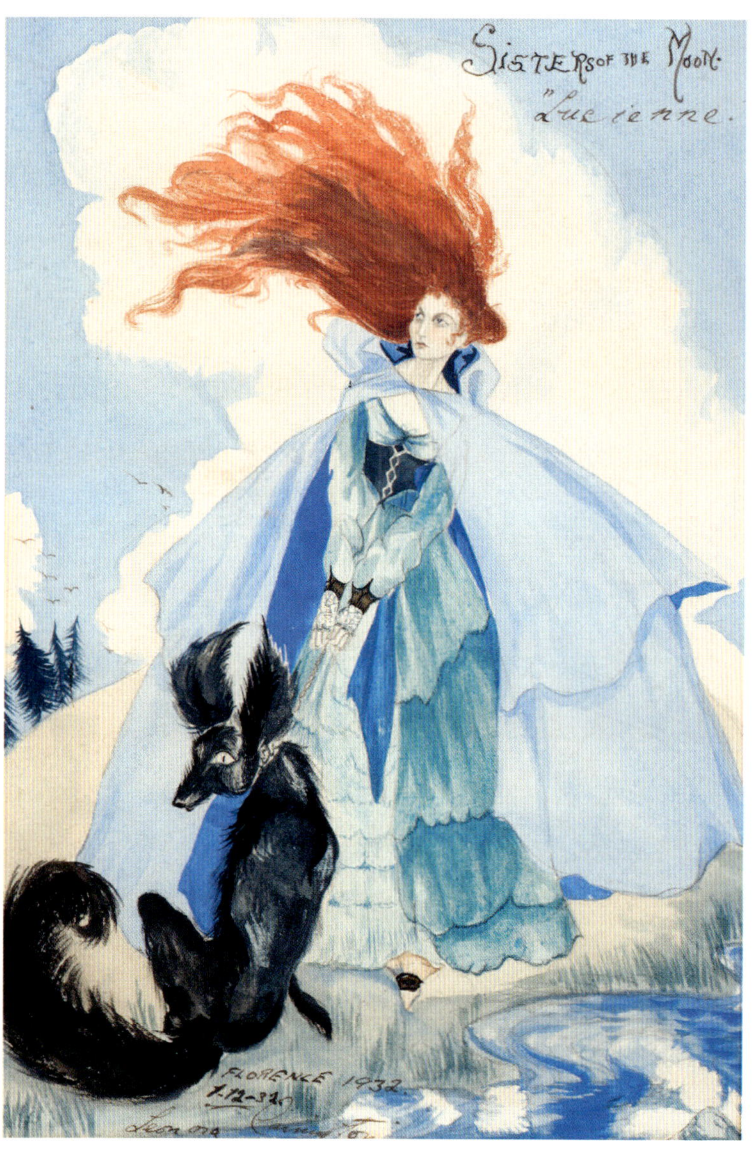

Leonora Carrington, *Sisters of the moon, Lucienne*, 1932. Watercolour, ink and graphite on paper.

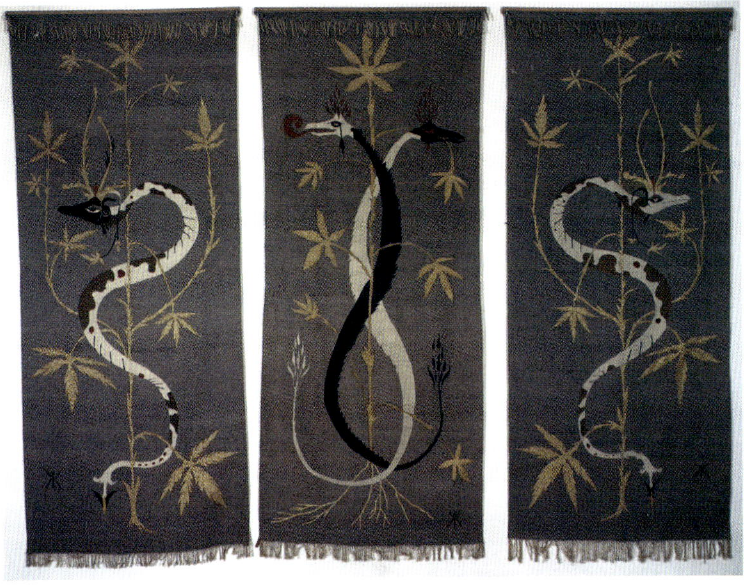

Leonora Carrington, *Las serpientes*, 1961. Wool and gold thread. 254 × 110 cm.

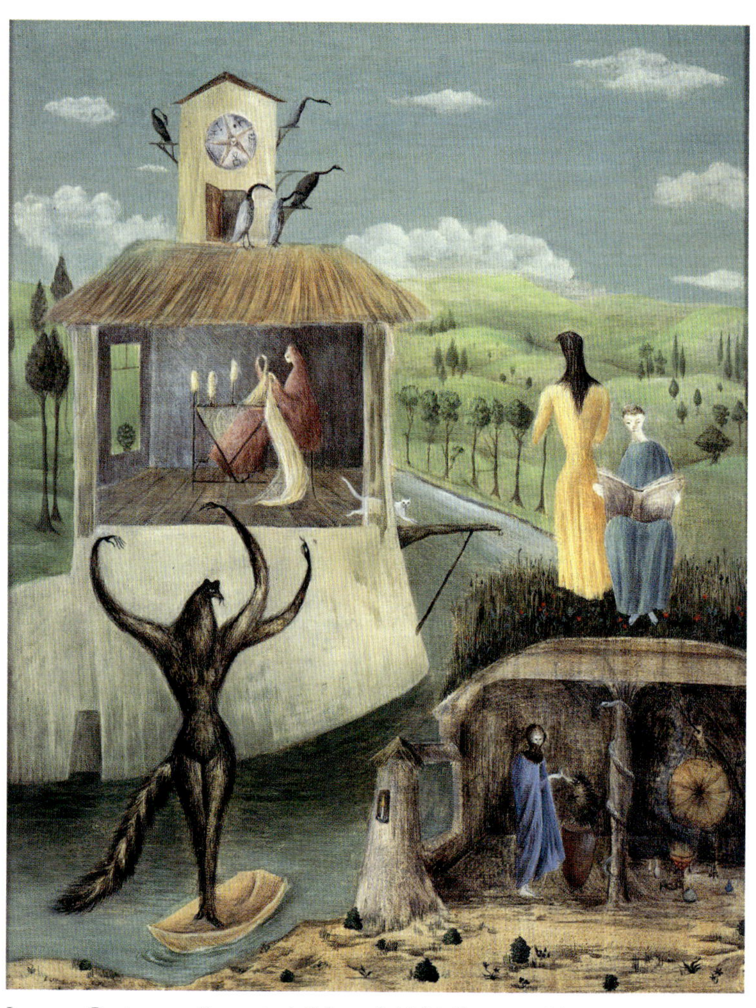

Leonora Carrington, *Seraputina's Rehearsal*, 1947. Casein on Masonite, 60 × 50 cm.

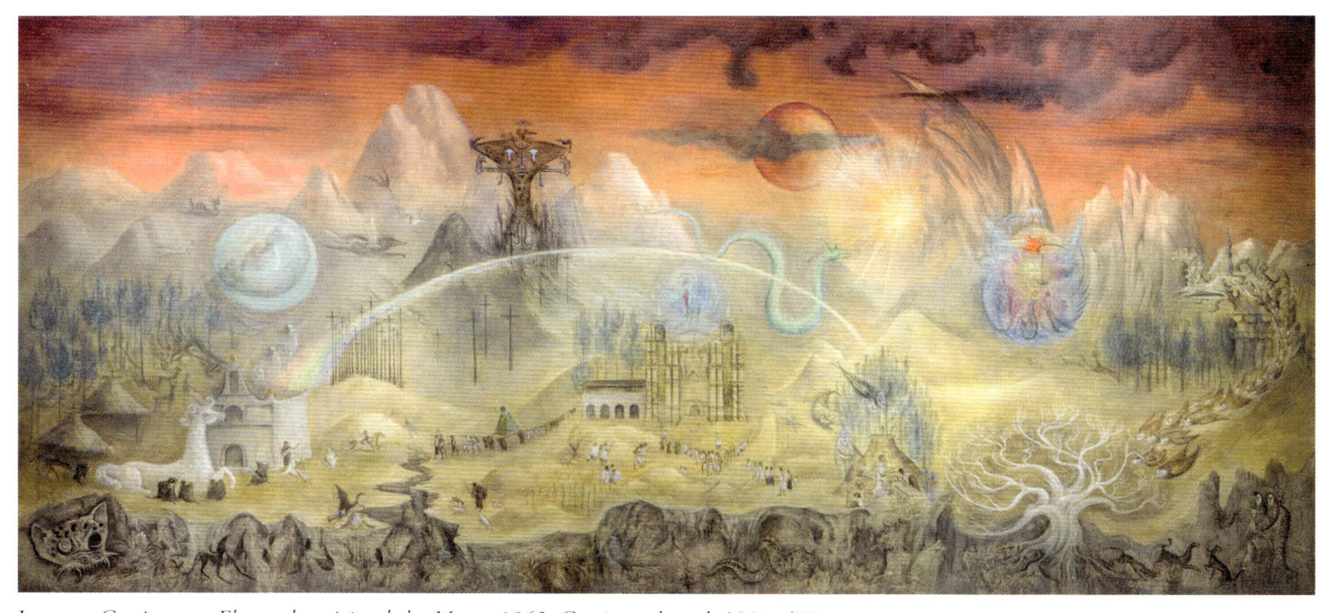

Leonora Carrington, *El mundo mágico de los Mayas*, 1963. Casein on board, 200 × 431 cm.

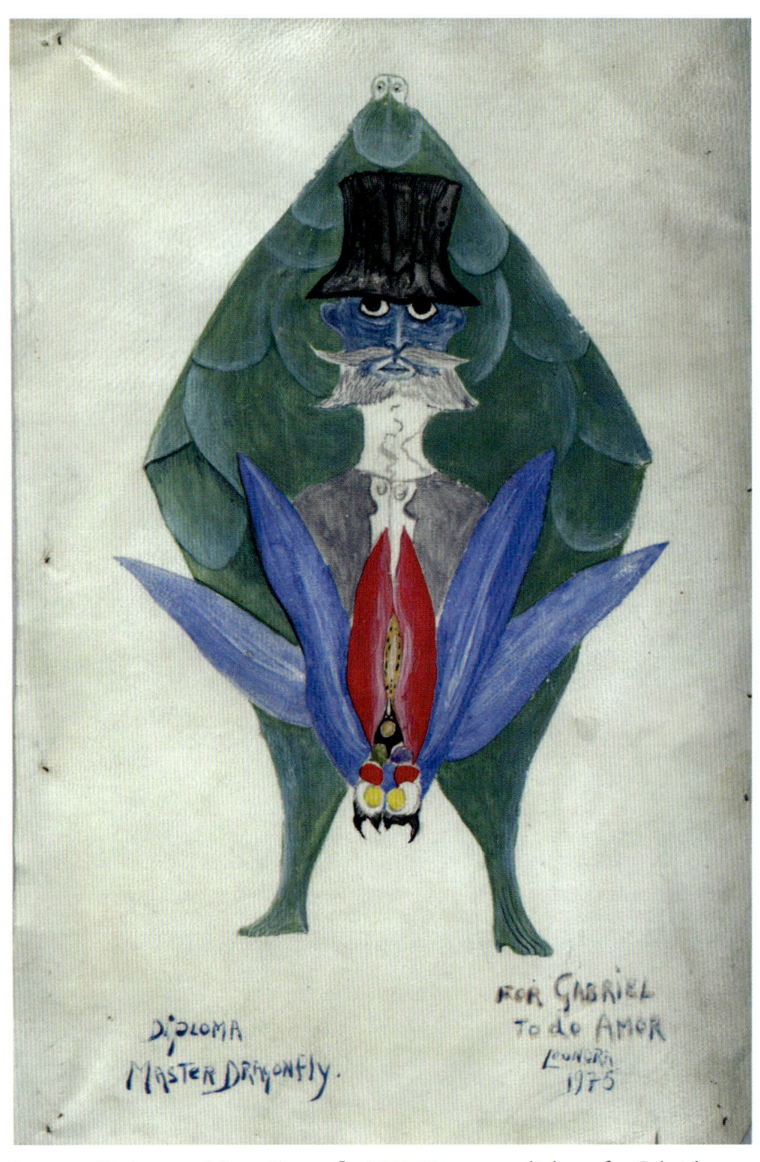

Leonora Carrington, *Master Dragonfly*, 1975. Humorous diploma for Gabriel Weisz. Casein on parchment.

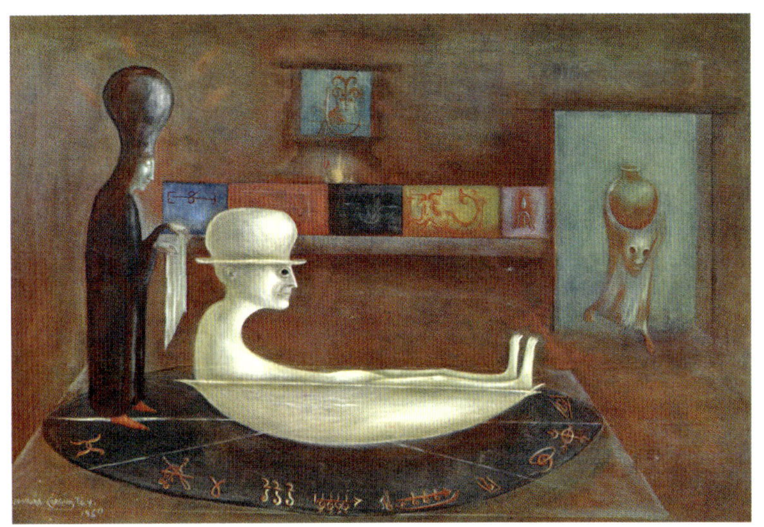

Leonora Carrington, *Rabbi Loew's Bath*, 1969. Oil on canvas, 45.5 × 68 cm.

After the rabbi
accomplished the practice
of his cabbalistic arts,
he whispered:
"My bath has gone cold",
Robertina, his daughter,
hastily brings hot water.
Esther, the beautiful wife
draws a towel steeped
in oriental essences.

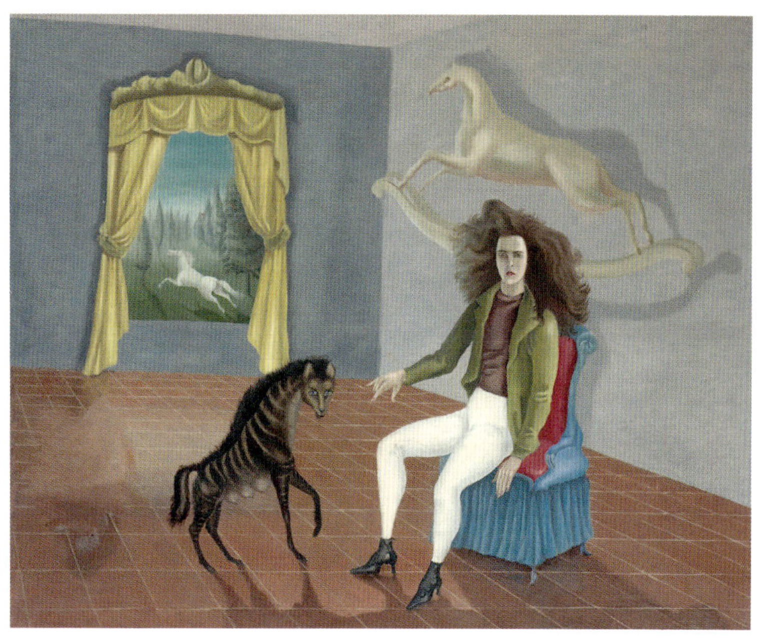

Leonora Carrington, *The Inn of the Dawn Horse* (self-portrait), 1937–38. Oil on canvas, 65.5 × 113 cm.

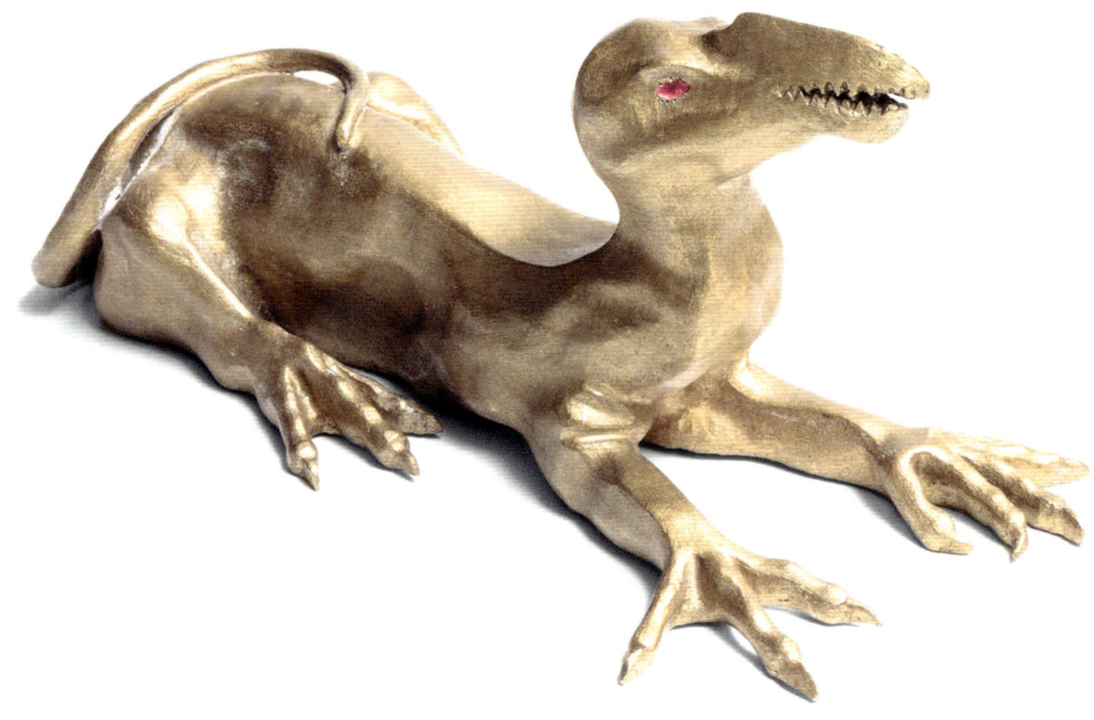

Leonora Carrington and Gabriel Weisz, *Sculpture-vulture*, 2010. Bronze, 28 × 13 × 14 cm.

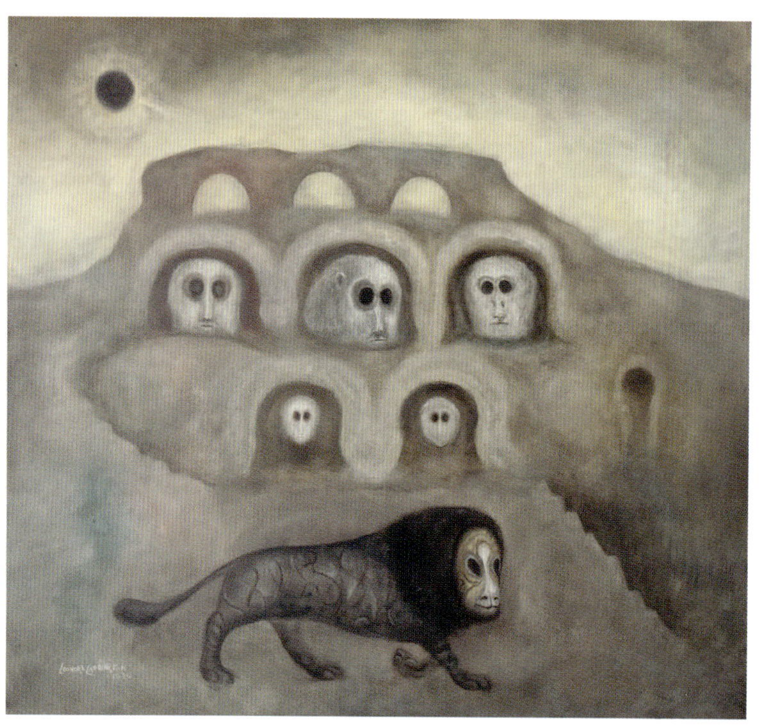

Leonora Carrington, *The Ancestor*, 1970. Oil on canvas, 90 × 100 cm.

The carbon eye Lion
prowls among ruins
in the Lemur Domain.
On that day
a moribund and blind sun
refused to warm over.

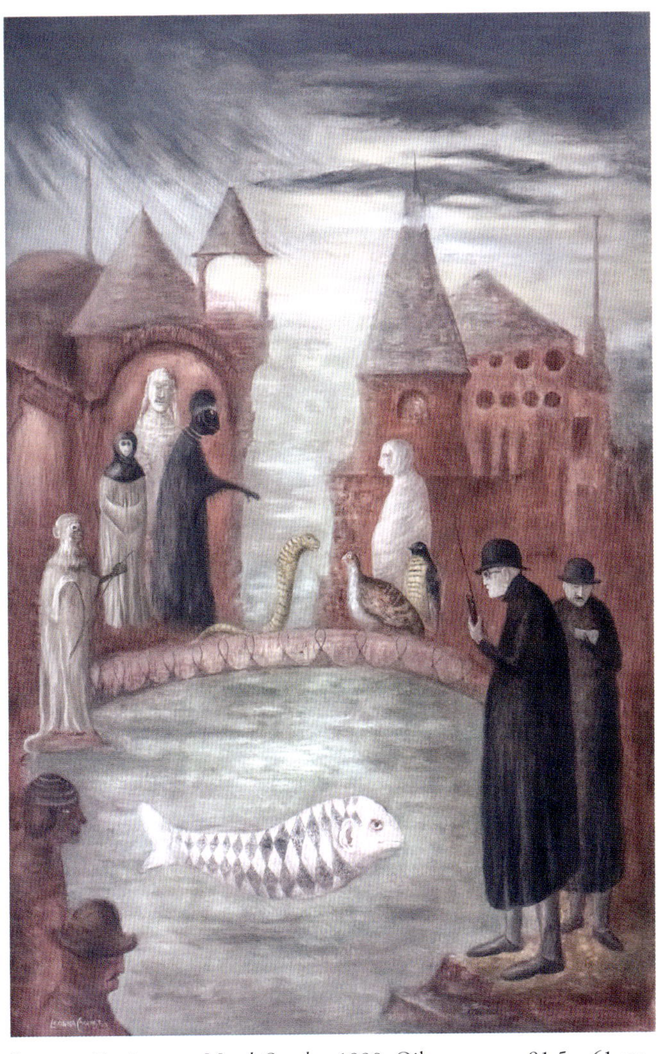

Leonora Carrington, *March Sunday*, 1990. Oil on canvas, 91.5 × 61 cm.

Who allowed Octropetrus,
the mosaic fish
to bathe in my pond?
Petrified voices invoke the serpents
and they cannot answer.

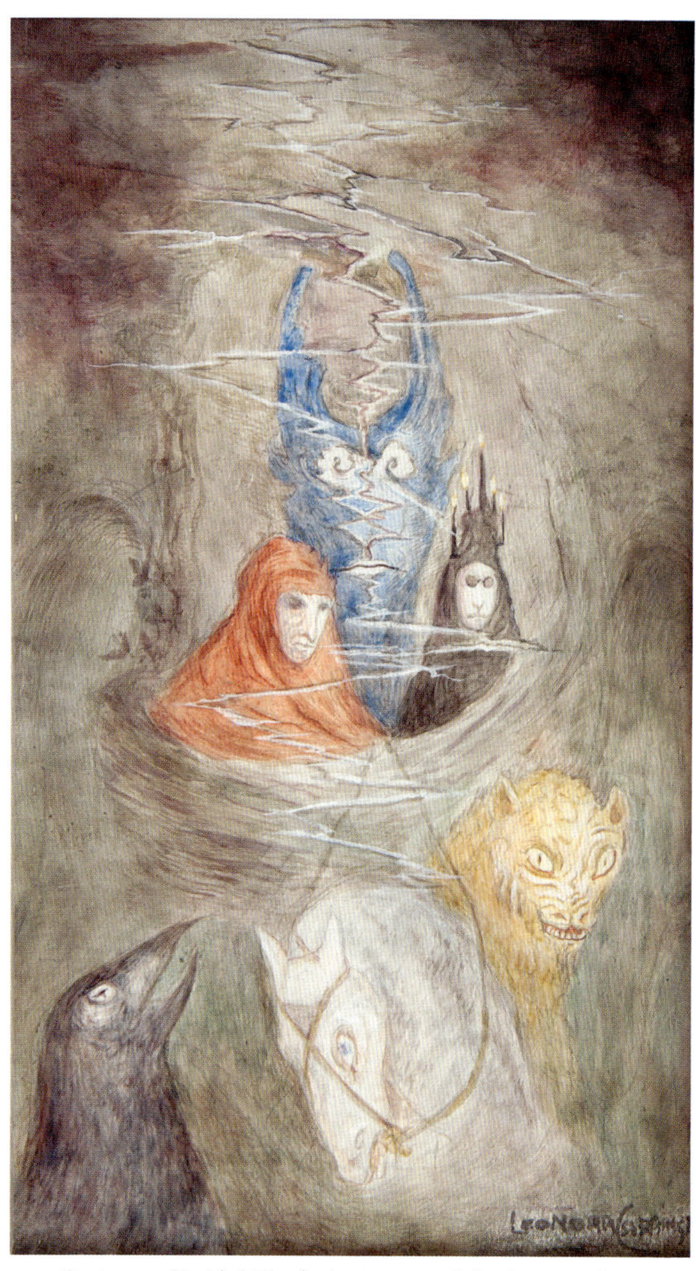

Leonora Carrington, Untitled. The final painting made by the artist. Casein on Masonite, 41.5 × 28.5 cm. n.d.

example of: she exhibited me as a complete reprobate. My class-mates whispered from one end of the room to the other. I kept my face neutral but hard; my role was to provide an opportunity for others to see what it is like to be a social leper. Leonora learned about the incident, and, as ever, became my ally. The next day she had a meeting with the headmistress. 'I thought this school followed a secular policy and respected a diversity of beliefs, as well as a lack of them', she told her. The next day the teacher who had punished me visited us at home. She had no choice but to apologise, though she didn't seem very enthusiastic about it.

Spanish grammar classes were particularly dry. My teacher's voice was monotonous, and I tried to hide my boredom between catnaps. Suddenly the teacher would begin to look shorter and shorter, her rat-like voice barely audible in the distance. She would begin to groom herself with her front paws as she explained the antepenultimate syllable accent. Verbs, nouns, and adjectives would all begin to grow very long tails.

After school I could wander at my leisure. There was a mysterious residence opposite our house, rumoured to be the home of Soviet spies, which naturally greatly increased its glamour and mystery. On one occasion, I managed to see the interior, having invented some excuse or other to enter. Inside, where I had expected to find intricate radio communication devices, there was a big crystal dome which let in plenty of light to a large empty room. My host, too, was a disappointment; he should have been sporting a Russian fur hat and a thick black moustache, but he was clean shaven and very kind to me. As the years went by, the property was eventually sold. The new owners knocked down the beautiful French-style house; however, the 1985 earthquake destroyed the nondescript building that replaced it. Its ruins were soon inhabited by squatters, who decorated the place with broken dolls and other motifs. It is amazing how drastically a place's identity can change in such a short space of time. One of the squatters soon came to be on good terms with my mother, and indeed with me. She was very watchful and had Leonora's house under permanent surveillance, so she would try to quiz me about the comings and goings of various visitors. I did not engage with this unsolicited gossip, but she would still always happily keep an eye on my car – the few pesos I gave her in return were always welcome. Whenever I asked about her health, she would always express concern about Leonora.

Like a chrysalis, and just like our memories, our home underwent its changes. I remember the time I was convinced there was buried treasure in the garden, only to find, after an enormous amount of digging, that the only thing down there was the drainage system. I also remember my father's darkroom on the way out to the patio. He was intent on teaching me photography, partly because of his unease about my lack of a profession. Chiki was like a magician in there, demonstrating how to expose negatives in near absolute darkness, illuminated only by a red light like the angry eye of a vulture or a Minotaur. We would load the film on to a metal reel to be developed, so that it wouldn't get scratched. As soon as I unloaded the film, it recoiled, like a good boa constrictor. The whole place had an acidic smell. As the film dried out, Chiki would take it over to the enlarger, his hands performing a kind of shadow theatre against the light projecting the negative on to the photographic paper.

The patio itself held the memory of other stories, like that afternoon in 1968 when we had to bury the mimeograph – a duplicating device that forced ink through a stencil on to sheets of paper, which we had been using to print anti-government propaganda in the basement. We were given a tip-off from a friend that the police were on their way to the house. The 'burial' was supposed to be a clandestine operation, but all the neighbours came out on to their roofs and peered down, making suggestions for how best to go about it.

Years later, I remained interested in transformative narratives and jumped at the opportunity to take on the role of stage director for a circus. Stage directors would generally refuse to help the circus people. Instead, I made it my business to keep the musicians and actors from fighting against the circus performers. I assembled the actors and musicians and told them that the people they despised often risked their lives for their art. 'Learn to respect their commitment.' One number opened with a rock singer riding a hippopotamus, and while at first she was a bit scared, she soon felt safe on the animal, and her singing got stronger and more confident. My intention was to combine theatre and pantomime with the circus. I invited the whole team over for dinner one night after the performance, and introduced them to Leonora, who was eager to meet them – she even prepared her famous 'bubble and squeak' with the leftovers from the previous day's roast. If I remember correctly, it was a young trapeze artist – a woman who did a stunt in which she hung extremely high up, with no safety net, from her very long hair – who whispered in a self–conscious voice that she sensed the presence of buried treasure under the kitchen floor. Everyone was surprised and discouraged when it became clear that Leonora was not particularly enthusiastic about the idea, politely declining their offer to help with the excavation enterprise.

One day my father came through the door announcing that he had bought us a glorious little present from a shop in the city's historic centre. He sat down at the table, and we had to finish lunch before we were allowed to see it. Finally, he asked me to bring him a glass of water, and to open all the windows to let some light into the room. He pulled from a bag what looked like scrunched-up balls of paper and threw two or three of them into the glass of water. Lo and behold, suddenly the glass transformed into an underwater garden with bright big flowers and exuberant vegetation. I spent hours admiring this aquatic paper garden, caught up in the exquisite sandal, rose, jasmine, and other fragrances that emerged from that minuscule universe.

Back in the Cuernavaca house, a pied-à-terre an hour's car journey away where we used to spend most weekends, Leonora planted a rose garden and covered the external pillars of the house in climbing jasmine that emitted an elegant fragrance every evening, as though the ghost of a woman were passing by. We often found scorpions running across the kitchen floor, and I would catch them with an empty glass and throw them out at the end of the garden where they could hide among the bamboos.

Our lunches at home were particularly interesting when Katy or her husband José came to visit. I remember José once stepped quickly over the threshold and revealed as many as ten expensive watches strapped up his forearms; each won in a different bet. Out of breath, and looking terrified, he asked Leonora to loan him some money, as he had lost everything in a game of cards. 'Of course', she replied. 'Just let me run to my room.' Leonora returned with a little envelope and handed it to José, who rushed out with it. We returned to our lunch, but it wasn't long before he was back. Leonora gave him a mischievous smile. It emerged that, instead of writing him a cheque, she had drawn a funny-looking cat, folded it up, and put it in the envelope. José wagged his finger at her. 'You are far more of a gypsy than I am!' he said.

José and Leonora did woodwork together; he was an accomplished carpenter. To this day, I still own a carved wooden doll that he made to Leonora's design – a she-wolf inlaid with abalone shells. They also made toys, among them a wooden roulette wheel on which Leonora painted some horses.

Earlier on I mentioned a trip to Liverpool with my son Daniel. The Tate had an exhibition of Leonora's work, in which was displayed a cradle, built by José and painted by Leonora, belonging to Katy and José's daughter Norah. Leonora decorated both sides of the crib: on one side there is a procession of giraffes and horses, plus a cat and other figures, all seemingly on a long journey towards the top end of the crib. On the opposite side, walking in the other direction, are two cats and a figure who seems to be greeting them. For Leonora, excursions and expeditions were always an important feature of her nomadic visions. Unfortunately, her work with José, who we had long since nicknamed 'El Niño', was brutally interrupted when he had a terrible accident, managing to chop his thumb off with an electric saw. Ever courageous, he wrapped his bloodied hand in a handkerchief and rushed himself to the hospital. I recall how his studio always smelled of sawdust.

Leonora worked with materials of all different kinds. I remember at one point she and my father tried their hands at tapestry. This new pursuit necessitated another major transformation of the house to accommodate two looms. They used a dyeing pot to dye the wool, and a spinning wheel to make the thread. After finishing my home-work, I would sit near the weaver, the ever-generous Mr Rosales, and listen to him tell traditional ghost stories as he worked the treadle and threw the shuttle housing the thread from one side to another. He pushed down the weft with a beater as the warp moved up and down, bringing the design to life. Leonora would trace her design on to a large piece of paper, and my father would cut it out and transfer it on to the weave. They chose different coloured wools and looked forward to seeing a finished tapestry after a couple of weeks' work. At first, their weavers told them that sophisticated designs were impossible to create – they should start with squares, rhom-buses, and simple circles. But Leonora had in mind the astonishing figurative complexity of the Gobelin tapestries she had admired in museums. Her and Chiki's ambition quickly grew, and working with the weavers, they stopped limiting themselves to geometric shapes and began to produce an incredible variety of complex designs. I remember the intricate intertwining of threads, from which emerged a series of visual stories. Each piece told a tale capable of conquering the mute whiteness of a blank wall (see Plate 7).

When it became apparent that the tapestries would not make money, and my parents had to remove the looms, Leonora dedi-cated herself to the arts of embroidery and appliqué, a stitching technique in which figures and scenes are represented by applying pieces of material to a larger piece of fabric that forms a base. She stitched each line on to layers of silk, linen, and denim. Leonora returned to these old techniques both to establish an artistic identity for herself and also as a kind of healing process, through which her inner demons would dissolve. She was also fascinated by dolls

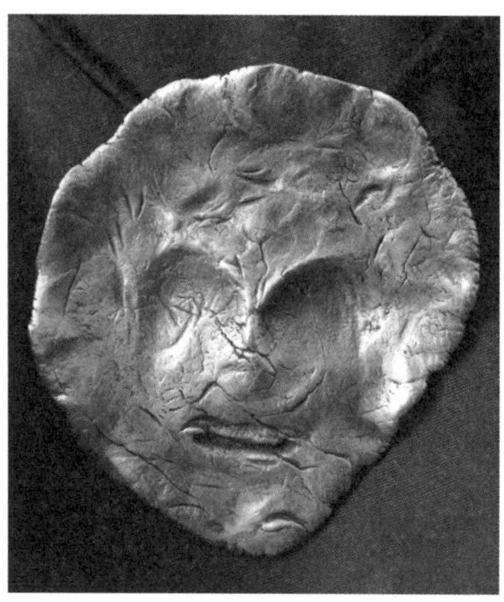

Leonora Carrington, silver pendant mask, n.d.

and puppets. I remember one doll of hers in particular, which had a head shaped from a peyote plant, to give her 'long dreams and a visionary nature'. This one, like all the others, was carefully crafted and stuffed with cat hair from her very own pets.

I hold in my hands, now, a little silver face she gave me, a woman's face. Leonora made her out of a piece of bee's wax: she pressed her thumbs in to create a nose and eyes; her fingernail carved out the mouth and lips; and then she took the piece of wax to the silversmith. This object demonstrates true mastery, the ability to create an expressive object with such economy of movement. Another creature she created for me, the White Goddess, hangs around my neck. It derives from an ivory hairbrush my grand-mother had given her, which slipped from her hand one day and broke its handle. Since she always had it in her to improvise and wanted to keep the object, she carved one side of the handle, in high relief, into the enigmatic face of a woman; on the other side, the face of an owl. I wanted to use it as a pendant, so we took it to a jeweller who set a ring in one end through which I could thread a leather cord. These objects are evidence of a creative persona, who we can only understand through her art. Leonora was more than the person present in our lives; she was also a creative character, a kind of visionary self who was the product of trial and error in a variety of artistic endeavours. These anecdotes, I hope, bring to light some aspects of Leonora's personal artistic history; her adventures in the transforming of different materials give us some insight into the nature of her imaginative interventions.

*

Occasionally Leonora would close the door to her room, and I would have to knock tentatively before entering. Something mysterious must be going on in there. 'Come in, but be careful', she would say, 'you can sit there but don't blow on anything near where I'm working.' She gestured to a painting she was about to adorn with gold leaf. She would remove the leaf – which would fly away at the slightest draught, so we had to avoid breathing on it too closely – from a small box using what was known as a squirrel hair brush. I felt as though the two of us were in an alchemical laboratory, complete with alembic to purify and separate liquids and a crucible to melt mysterious substances. She first deposited the leaf on the gilding pad, a little cushion covered with soft suede leather. There it was cut to the desired size, guarded by three small parchment panels to protect it from any air currents. It looked like a miniature stage on which something momentous was about to happen. Leonora used an agate burnisher to seal and polish the surface. The golden moth would alight on the painting, trapped forever in its gluey bed, bestowing on the work a special light that somehow also ignited our senses.

It was in 1960 that Leonora accepted another project that animated the house on Calle Chihuahua once more, making it buzz with activity. Alejandro Jodorowsky, a Chilean who had worked as a mime in France with Marcel Marceau, staged her play *Pénélope*. I remember Leonora kneeling over a bucket full of long newspaper strips we had cut up. On a table stood a chicken wire structure suggesting the rough shape of a horse's head, which, thinking back, initially seemed hideous to me. We glued the strips to the chicken wire, covering the entire surface in multiple layers. Slowly, the shape of Tartarus began to emerge, the rocking horse that comes to life at the beginning of the play, a character Leonora first dreamt up in the nursery as a child. I loved this experience of creating objects that animated the written word; it had a huge impact on me. An array of mysterious, rustic materials turns into props: objects devoted to bringing dramatic fiction to life in a palpable way. Leonora guided me with precision and dexterity, introducing me to new art forms, mutating shapes and materials, pushing back against their resistance to becoming something that they were not until they eventually took on the shape she wanted. During the rebirth of her written text as an astonishing visual phenomenon, those ephemeral props whose existence was so short-lived were nevertheless able to open up, in the hands of performers, the emotional responses of each audience member. As for me, the work of helping to build Tartarus's powerful head helped develop my tactile imagination. My hands learned the hidden secrets of different materials as I shaped them into objects. As I worked, in my imagination the nursery in *Pénélope* was telescoped into a sun-filled, many-windowed chamber; that little recess in the house on Calle Chihuahua became a paradise for cats and dogs, who lay enjoying the warmth, their delicate bellies moving rhythmically up and down. Then suddenly the animals were gone, hidden somewhere. The smell of glue was overpowering once more, and the room went back to being a store for theatre props, a workshop where fantastic creatures were brought to life, destined for a new existence on stage, with all the energy centring on Tartarus.

In between our chores, Leonora and I exchanged ideas about how to build some object or other. The workshop had a small electric cooking stove that served to boil up the carpenter's glue and Blanco de España or whiting, which acquired a thick consistency when it was ready. We painted Tartarus with this mixture until all the unevenness and imperfections were covered up. When we applied the papier mâché to the chicken wire, our hands grew scaly and reptilian, requiring us to pull off a second skin once we'd finished. We were human usurpers of divine power, animating structures like gods and goddesses, directing our creations of new life towards the stage. Whoever took on the role of Tartarus would wear the sculpted head, giving it a voice and movements. From that modest piece of chicken wire covered in a skin of hardened glue and paper there emerged a magnificent creature, a white stallion that transformed all understandings of what it meant to be a horse. Time, for me, became unimportant, conquered by this creative activity. These were moments dedicated only to play – nothing else could get in the way. One night I woke up to find that Tartarus had acquired a poetic presence in my room. His white head was gently bathed in moonlight, defying the darkness. As we slept, the spectral horse became the new master of the workshop.

When the opening of *Pénélope* was finally upon us, we were disappointed to learn that the government censors had deemed it appropriate only for adults. It seemed ironic that a play that

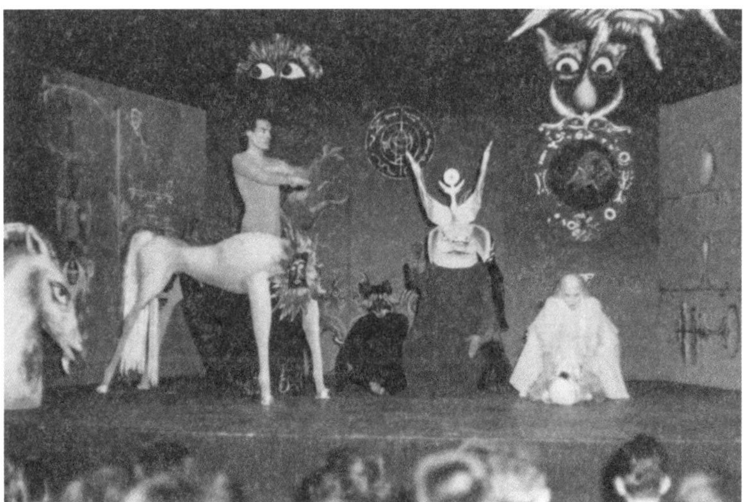

Mise en scène, Pénélope. Photo: Chiki Weisz.

belonged to Leonora's childhood was denied precisely this part of its identity. Since at the time I was only a teenager, I wasn't able to attend the opening night. I still feel that the play belongs to me in some way, though. The work I did preparing the set became part of my identity; it gave me a way of inhabiting imagination. The intense attention to detail necessary to create the stage horse's simultaneous visibility and vulnerability, as well as the pleasure we experienced through the sheer play of putting him together – this is how creative memories are shaped, how creative bodies are informed. In some situations, stagecraft can transform our psyche.

Leonora and I would have laughed together at an article about *Pénélope* I recently stumbled upon in a French magazine called *Docsur*, which was interested in Surrealism and had a limited print run of 150 copies. It documents the staging of the play by the 'Unfinished Theatre' company at the Chapelle Expiatoire on the rue Pasquier in Paris, and recounts how the Duke Alphonse d'Anjou and Cádiz, cousin to Juan Carlos of Spain and head of the Borbón House, declared publicly that the play was an insult to the Chapelle Expiatoire. The Duke, who admitted not having personally attended the performance, is said to have declared, 'It seems to me out of place and inappropriate to stage a performance of this nature. I fully understand the legitimate emotions suffered by several people in response to the serious profanation it contained.' The article goes on:

Last Thursday the Duke Alphonse d'Anjou and Cádiz criticized *Pénélope*, a Surrealist play by Leonora Carrington [...] and on Friday a group of demonstrators interrupted the performance. On Tuesday night, royalists and Catholic traditionalists destroyed the set, a costume, some of the lighting equipment, and recordings of France Culture.[21]

---

[21] Christian Charrière, 'Review of *Pénélope*', *Docsur: Documents sur le surréalisme*, 1 (1986).

I could barely believe what I was reading. It felt like something out of the nineteenth century, even though this happened in 1986. The mob of traditionalists and royalists were upset because only a few steps from the Chapelle Expiatoire theatre was the tomb of Louis XVI, whose spirit, they assumed, would have been offended by Leonora's art. The reactionary French newspaper *Figaro*, for its part, considered *Pénélope* to be a 'sexual and sadomasochistic play'.[22] These libellous statements from enraged individuals scarcely conceal the biases of their authors. How tragic it must be to live with such an acute lack of humour. Nevertheless, though their indignation is laughable, it's important not to lose sight of the fact that this kind of regressive, even repressive behaviour is encountered even today.

As I continue to tell these stories about Leonora through various objects and works that she created, I want to return to the period when I worked with a circus. The kinds of performances we staged were a hybrid of theatrical and circus acts. Leonora was in charge of design, creating, for example, an outstanding dragon-vehicle from which a legless contortionist leapt. In the original act, this poor fellow had leapt out of a filthy cloth sack; when he saw Leonora's new design, he could scarcely believe his luck.

In 1973 the novice director Juan López Moctezuma had invited both Leonora and me to plan and build the sets for his film *Mansion of Madness*, based on the work of Edgar Allan Poe. In this way, I secured a writing credit to add to my already existing credits for production and design. Leonora and I played around with ideas, which I later elaborated on set. The cameraman despised me because he disapproved of the sets I built. For instance, I arranged for some scenes to be shot in the Museo Chopo, a former natural history museum that was at the time completely abandoned, with empty cabinets and exhibition halls. I improvised by covering large surfaces with *zacate*, a type of grass often used as a scourer, to

[22] Ibid.

create the effect of volume and texture in the space. I also stumbled upon a collection of animal skulls and other bones, which I hung up to create a kind of macabre throne. I handed out taxidermy animals – what remained of a heterogeneous collection previously displayed in the museum – to the actors, who used them as make-shift musical instruments. I also wrote some of the dialogue for the film. Anything was possible in this playground offered to me by Leonora, who refused ever to appear on set herself.

Forever generous, she included me in a whole series of projects in this way – or I would include her. One such project was the film *El dominio encantado o el Encanto dominado* (*The Enchanted Domain or Dominated Enchantment*). However, I never managed to get my hands on a copy of this film, because the producer who financed the work claimed to have created the entire thing himself. Leonora and I articulated the film's universe through poetry and some of her childhood objects, including a Tarot set and an assort-ment of small, delicately painted brass animals she had brought with her from England – her English background was always present in our home – such that the film operates as a mnemonic device for things that were central to our lives. However, since my part in its creation was never acknowledged, the film has become hidden, for me, behind a veil of loss, and I can barely remember it – a distant dream. Still, Leonora and I were constantly discussing different pro-jects, and these conversations fuelled in me the need to create.

*

Some time ago, I was reflecting on the role of the dining table in the lives of refugees. For us, the table where I sit now was a meet-ing ground where we discussed politics and art as well as the more trivial details of our day-to-day existence, all the while sharing food, each of us serving ourselves from the kitchen. It was a place where we could establish our identities and share the challenges life brought us. During these meals, we would choose whichever words best expressed what we wanted to say; sometimes, those words would be in Spanish, sometimes in English or French, as each language carried its emotional substance. We referred to this mixture as 'volapük', a term coined in the nineteenth century by Johann Martin Schleyer to describe a mixture of English, German, and French. If only I could go back and be a fly on the wall during those long-ago conversations between Edward James, Luis Buñuel, Aldous Huxley, Octavio Paz, Remedios Varo, Wilfredo Lam, Alice Rahon, and all the others who at one point or other sat around this very same table, enjoying themselves, gossiping and laughing.

It was at this table that we planned our family trip to Xilitla, that palace where Edward James spent his time writing poems, having surrounded himself with extravagant objects and exotic animals. It is shocking for visitors to experience the brusque interruption of the exuberant vegetation by concrete palm trees painted in loud colours, which I imagine whispering defiantly, *We are artificial! We are artificial!* Up above, a flock of parrots squawk past, leaving a trace of green in the sky; blindingly white cockatoos interrupt their conversations. This place is an Eden on the brink of madness, a fairy tale set in an impenetrable, exotic jungle. James fills the space with the stories he imagines, living out his dream world and expressing himself through that wonderful artistic domain mastered by Rousseau, Magritte, Leonora, and so many others. The palace at Xilitla is reminiscent of the work of Ferdinand Cheval, a French postman who collected stones and pieces of broken porcelain over the course of thirty-three years before building the *Palais idéal* in Hauterives, bringing to life the building he had seen in a vision.[23] Leonora, always happy to fashion imaginary landscapes, needed little persuading to paint a daunting fresco of a she-goat reclining against a column, to guard the entrance to one of James's mysterious gardens.

[23] See Paul Soldner, 'The Fantastic Palace of Ferdinand Cheval', *Craft Horizons*, 28.1 (1968), pp. 9–19.

Whenever he came through Mexico City, James would stay at the Hotel Francis on Paseo de la Reforma – an establishment that still exists today, although it goes by another name. He would pay us visits accompanied by a whole menagerie of creatures he had either purchased or adopted on his trips to South America. He emerged from a taxi, after one such trip, carrying perforated cardboard boxes that contained a score of patient iguanas waiting to be released. We let them out on the terrace of the Calle Chihuahua house, and they crawled around slowly on their prehistoric legs, enjoying the fierce sunlight, their scaly necks erect and elegant as Quetzalcoatls. Every rendezvous with James brought something unexpected. I doubt Leonora was much amused, though, the time that both the dining room and kitchen were colonised by an indeterminate number of ill-tempered *tejones* – Mexican badgers – which proceeded to def-ecate left, right, and centre and distribute painful bites to anyone who dared approach them. James washed his hands obsessively and wandered the house like a masculine reincarnation of Lady Macbeth. He would lie down on any available bed – at dusk, you could make out his goatee pointing up to the ceiling like the effigy of a Chaldean emperor prostrated on a stone tomb. Leonora often reminisced about one particular time when James invited her out for dinner:

He took me to an expensive restaurant, but once dinner was over, he started to look dismayed, frantically pulling out one envelope after another, each containing just a few peso bills. He eventually announced, with apparent frustration, that he'd left his money at the hotel. Well, I responded, we'd better get washing dishes, then, or it'll be jailtime for us.

He did, she told me, eventually manage to pay the bill.

Edward James wrote a preface for Leonora's exhibition at the Pierre Matisse gallery in New York, in the early spring of 1948. He suggested that Leonora's paintings underwent a radical change after the year 1945. A good stretch of time after, when I was at the Tate Liverpool exhibition, accompanied by Daniel, we confirmed what James surmised. We noticed that her early paintings, which seemed to depict fairytale worlds, were quite different from her later paintings, which, with their more sophisticated thematic elements, helped build her imaginative niche. As she developed her art, my mother discovered a way of expressing her imaginary landscapes through art, and as a result, her paintings became more personal and pictorially unique. She now owned her visual language.

In the autumn of 1945, Leonora invited James to her workshop. He remarked that the more sumptuous the workshop, the more diminished the artistic result. Leonora's workplace, he wrote, was 'small in the extreme. An ill-furnished and not very well-lit room. It had nothing to endow it with the title of a studio at all, save a few almost worn-out paint brushes and a number of gesso panels' – that is, a white material originally used in medieval times as a prepared base on which to paint with a fast-drying combination of tempera and egg yolks. James continued: 'The place was a combined kitchen, nursery, bedroom, kennel and junk-store.' As the years went by, little about the character of Leonora's studio changed, even when she had enough money to make adjustments to the house. It had an austere concrete platform where one would find different bottles, paint boxes, brushes, and tubes of oil paint. Climbing plants grew over the walls, and dolls painted in unfinished acrylic hung from the ceiling. An easel stood in the centre of the room, accompanied by a wooden chair with a woven wicker seat, where she would sit facing the canvas. You can still detect the faint smell of varnish, and a mixture of turpentine, beeswax, and resin. In his role as spectator, James describes Leonora's work as containing half-mythological, half-peasant figures, the enamelled brilliance of whose garments looms out from soft, mossy grounds of grey and buff and green. Between them, they compose ghostly scenes which might have been better comprehended by, and more familiar to, spectators in the fifteenth or sixteenth centuries.

In his preface, James points out the unique place Leonora's work occupies in the history of English art, in stark contrast to the lack of appreciation she received in Mexico. He also touches on another important aspect of her art, which is her sense of humour. This sense often manifested as a friendly or sarcastic interaction with her imaginary characters. An exchange between James and my mother reveals precisely what she was reaching for:

'I was in her studio last April when she was painting the picture called *Seraputina's Rehearsal*', James remarked. She had just begun painting a fragile little boat (see Plate 8).

She turned to James, and asked, 'What colour shall I make the boat?'

'Why not paint it white', he replied, 'with rows of black spots, so that it will look as if it was folded newspaper, like a cocked hat.'

'That would be nice', she answered, 'but it would be too humorous.'

It is clear to me, reading this exchange, that my mother sought a careful balance between poetic humour, which is not accessible at first glance, and a less sophisticated and more mundane kind of humour. James concludes his account of my mother's work by admiring Leonora's tempera paintings, referring to 'the bird-subtle nuances in the lights and plumage of her pictures [...] the rhythm and tone', and 'the professionally perfect technique of her tempera colours'.[24] These statements about a certain bird-like spirit perfectly express that volatile, ghostly quality found in much of her work – it is the kind of atmosphere one most often senses in a dream.

I think back to my adolescence and that glittering look that appeared in Leonora's eye when we first travelled to Europe by train, via Saint Louis and New York. I am engrossed in a book, having begun my travels well-equipped with a whole collection of Jules Verne given to me by Chiki. The rocking cadence of the train relaxes me, and as the landscape passes by out of the window it

---

[24] Manuscript from my personal archive.

is somehow incorporated into my reading. As we leave the station, we abandon all routine. Emotion and excitement charge our arrival in New York. We head to the Village in search of a hotel and are shown some rooms by a clerk. When Leonora pulls back the bedsheets, there scurries out a cockroach so large that she belongs in the ranks of mythological creatures – we agreed that she bore a greater resemblance to a cat than an insect, given her considerable corpulence. As we walk out into the corridor, a young woman with very dirty hair and sporting many small, tinkling bells, limps past us, dragging her unforgettable mirror image: an equally filthy, limping dog.

While we were there, Marcel Duchamp invited us to his apartment. He addressed me first, wanting to know if I would like to play. Without waiting for an answer, he pulled up a chair and sat me down in front of a chess board. With absolutely no change in his expression – a rather distant look – he pushed the button on a chess timer and left me to make the first move while he went off to entertain his other guests. Needless to say, I lost within only a few moves of his very bony fingers. That game was the only contact I ever had with that celebrated, unknown character, and he retained for me the enigmatic aura of an adult, captive in a glass box, cloaked in silence.

When the New York sojourn came to an end, we boarded the SS *United States*, an ocean liner bound for Europe. On the trip, I met a Sikh boy who I quickly befriended. I was fascinated by the way he and his father arranged their beautiful, glossy dark hair in turbans. The boy's father also used a special net to keep his moustache and beard in place, impressing me with his elegance. It was only two days, though, before a storm hit us. I was delighted, rushing to and fro down the corridors. In the dining room, it was amusing to find that the chairs slid around as though under the force of a giant magnet, or as though a magician hidden behind heavy curtains was playing tricks on us, making objects come to life. One lady screamed and fell to the floor. Outside, giant green waves reached incredible heights, spewing foam from their open jaws, and rain battered furiously at the windows. I remember being jolted from side to side, trying to grip the handrail. Leonora's face was very pale, and it wasn't long before she succumbed to nausea and had to retire to her cabin. I was dying to have a peek at the swimming pool, a miniature imitation of the sea with water splashing up on to the walls on all sides. The waves continued to reach huge heights, washing over the deck, but the floating city advanced undeterred.

When we finally arrived, we took a train from France to Switzerland in order to learn how to ski. The snow was always a source of wonder for me. I gazed out of the window of the train's dining car at all those mountains clad in glittering white robes. Once there, it quickly became clear that our hotel was far too elegant for both our tastes and our pockets. The controls for the bathtub resembled an aeroplane cockpit: a complex assortment of gleaming buttons for temperature control and water pressure. Coming out of the bathroom, you found every kind of essence on display – not to mention enough soap for a small army. The restaurant, meanwhile, was very pretentious, with food that was a bit too exotic for us. Guests would dress up for dinner, the waiters set knives and forks like surgical instruments beside each plate. In contrast, we looked rather like gypsies, so much so that the *maître d'* looked at us as though we were something he had just fished out of the rubbish bin. He sat us at a table behind a large column where none of the other diners could scrutinise us. From where I was sitting, I watched an impeccably dressed young man whisper something to what looked like one of his daughters. He was gesturing to the way the silver was laid out on the table, introducing her to one of the many rituals of the bourgeoisie.

Early the next morning, we headed out on to the mountain to begin our skiing lessons with a good and very patient instructor. In the afternoon, we took refuge in a small café, where three rather decrepit, fragile-looking musicians played melancholically on their instruments. One of them wore a jacket that was far too large for him. We had an exceptionally good hot chocolate that I can still taste to this day. I was wearing a hat with all sorts of metallic insignia on it, which also included a toy seal, a gift destined for a girlfriend who would come to meet me when I arrived back in Mexico City. I must have looked like some sort of distinguished shaman, though I was, in fact, a good deal less interesting. We stayed at the hotel for a couple more days before Leonora confided in me that we were running out of money. 'I'm afraid our only option is to escape in the night, take a taxi out of town and board the train one station over', she told me. Thus, our adventure as fugitives began, and the pretentious hotel was left behind. From a distance, it looked like a slightly over-decorated wedding cake.

Leonora wanted to visit her mother, so we travelled to London. Long gone were the mansions and servants of her childhood; my grandmother now lived in a flat. I was looking forward to meeting my uncles, excited by the novelty of family I barely knew. Leonora, however, was impatient to visit the city's museums, and once there asked repeatedly to know what I thought. She allowed me to explore on my terms, but also devised activities for me, encouraging me to seek out different items and imagine what each character or creature in a painting might be thinking. Leonora intervened in my musings with questions or remarks, but never tried to guide me in my interpretations. My mother was a great teacher, demonstrating gently how the Flemish masters exposed textures and combined their colours artfully. Van Eyck and Bruegel, she explained, belonged to an era of great discovery and self-knowledge: 'Bruegel the Elder and his infinite landscapes. He was a master image-maker with a fondness for hallucinatory scenes.' In her enthusiasm, at one point she got too close to a painting, tracing its tones of lightness and dark in the air, and it wasn't long before an attendant, who had been nervously following us around, warned us to keep our distance. Most of the time, Leonora encouraged me to understand art through my body, intuitively, unencumbered by grandiose intellectual explanations. 'What do you feel?' She had studied many of these paintings when she was an art student and had undertaken extensive visual training, poring over different ways of representing poses, expressions, hand gestures, animals, vegetation, and a whole repertoire of objects. She knew the virtuosity required to depict the illusion of glass objects, with all their translucent tonalities, shadows, and other wonders of light and darkness; she knew the enigmatic skill necessary to create real art. She understood the shape of horses, their special personalities, their musculature, the position of their legs, how to represent speed, freezing a single fleeting moment in time. We spent some time considering the work of Joseph Mallord William Turner, who created an extraordinary range of hues that I can still see if I close my eyes. Turner, a British landscape romantic from the nineteenth century, opened the door to Impressionism with his bleary skies and left a legacy as a master illuminator. He was known for his watercolours, and I often still think about those liquid landscapes of his.

While we were in the UK, Leonora also wanted to visit Roland Penrose, who lived in Sussex with Lee Miller, at Farley House. He took us to Brighton Pier, where I made friends with Penrose's son Tony, playing with him for hours on end on the slot machines. Penrose was an English Surrealist who first began to make an impact on the British artistic scene with his International Surrealist Exhibition in London in 1936. In the years after the war, he went on to transform the country's entire artistic panorama.[25] Miller, meanwhile, was one of the most important photographers of the twentieth century. Her photographs revealed the true meaning of war while playing with Surrealist themes, and she did much to document the most important figures of the Surrealist movement.

Back in Mexico one boring afternoon, Leonora picked up the phone to Alice Rahon, who invited us over to her house. Alice, a poet and painter, was married to the Surrealist artist Wolfgang

[25] For more on Roland Penrose, see the 'International Surrealism' section of Marcel Jean, *The Autobiography of Surrealism: The Documents of Twentieth-Century Art* (New York: Viking Press, 1980), p. 363.

Palen, through whom she also met Breton. She was waiting for us outside her house when we got out of the taxi; inside, she made us a cup of tea and introduced us to a friend who wanted to show us a film he had made. In it, ferocious dinosaurs paraded around on the screen, traversing volcanic landscapes. He had built the animated creatures out of rubber and adjusted each of their poses between frames. The resulting movements were choppy; the dinosaurs reacted in slow motion, and the film seemed interminable to me. I found his explanations of how he had created the scale models and sets far more interesting.

Leonora prepared a few sketches for a work of art which was intended to become a mural to be displayed at Mexico City's Oncology Hospital, but the muralist David Alfaro Siqueiros arrogated the project. Nevertheless, the Anthropological Museum soon commissioned Leonora to create another mural, and she took herself off to the state of Chiapas to do some research. While there, Leonora found inspiration in the sacred Maya book *Popol Vuh* and befriended a Zinacantan *curandero* or healer. I am able to examine each of the sketches she prepared for this project in the book *El mundo mágico de los Mayas*.[26] She filled notebook after notebook with delicate sketches – of hummingbirds and the 'House of Bats' or 'Totilmelil', and of places such as Amatenango del Valle, a magnificent market in front of a white church – that were to become part of the larger artwork (see Plate 9). Much of the final mural's charm lies in the animals it represents, which throb with life; it includes a carefully rendered jaguarundi, a tapir, weasels, monkeys, and birds noisily spreading their wings. Elsewhere, women wrap their children to their bodies using *rebozos* and Chamula people hurry towards their destinations, their braided hair flying out behind them. The mural depicts the *nahuales*, those quasi-humans capable of transforming into beasts at will. We can see a

[26] See Leonora's notes on the sketches for *El mundo mágico de los Mayas*, Instituto Nacional de Antropología e Historia, 1st edn (Ciudad de México: SEP, 1964).

scorpion in combat with a bolt of lightning, perhaps representing Scorpio, the well-known Maya constellation. Slightly higher up we find a tree full of animals: an owl-person, horned serpents, a *chac-mool* lying vigilant. These details are interwoven with one another in a palette of intense blacks, whites, and many other colours, creating a seductive whole that attracts a great number of spectators every year. However, Leonora's muralism avoids monumentality as is the trait among Mexican *muralistas.*

Daniel and I saw the mural at the Tate exhibition in Liverpool. From a distance, the blur of colour seems to endow the painting with movement, demanding the spectator's attention. The exhibition was bursting with Leonora's work, but the mural was the piece that opened the exhibition. As you looked at it, you could practically hear the dogs barking, and the vendors selling their wares, and smell the fruit, vegetables, raw meat, and copal incense – it seemed to pour directly out of the wall. The *curandero* Leonora had befriended was sadly murdered some months after her visit to Chiapas after he was unable to cure somebody's family member. As I looked at the mural, I felt that my mother had posthumously captured his spirit in the healing ceremony she depicted there.

I follow the mosaic of my memories back to Mexico and remember my youthful encounter with Renato Leduc, who had been instrumental in my mother's escape from the mental institution and a Europe battered by war and violence. Leduc contacted me when I was at university and asked whether I had ever been to the Café Habana, a place known for vibrant political debate, where Fidel and Che had once been frequent visitors. Leonora must have asked Leduc to take me out for a cup of coffee and advise me to stay out of trouble. We sat down in the café to talk politics, and he gave me some tips on how to conduct myself at a demonstration against the war in Vietnam that I was planning to attend. Combing his fingers through a shock of white hair, and offering me a cigarette, he warned that I should always be alert to how other people were behaving. 'Be on the look-out for those police assholes dressed as civilians', he said before we finished our drinks and said our goodbyes. For a while, I had been attending meetings of a group of young anarchists. They couldn't understand my desire to attend a demonstration organised by communists, even when I remonstrated that I could not condition my anti-war stance by the ideological orientation of the protest's organisers. Leonora felt reassured by my chat with Leduc, believing I was at less risk of being arrested. As it turned out, though, and as Leduc had warned might happen, plainclothes police charged at us at the demonstration and beat us with metal rods rolled up inside newspapers. I was lucky to escape with only minor injuries on my back, but the pain remained, an indelible tattoo to remind me of the brutality of the police. I ran off through the streets of the historic centre until I finally felt safe enough to dash into a café, catch my breath, and shakily drink a coffee until I judged a sufficient amount of time had elapsed.

When I was younger, Leonora paid for a couple of private tuition sessions to improve my grades in chemistry at school. The teacher was a young Peruvian woman who had recently escaped her country after becoming involved in an anti-government resistance movement. Those chemistry sessions had an interesting twist to them, as I managed to persuade my teacher to reluctantly give me some insight into how to build a rocket. Our testing ground was the terrace of the house on Calle Chihuahua, and those most affected by our clandestine activities were my mother and two beautiful green parrots. After every detonation Leonora would scream 'What are you doing?!', and the two terrified parrots would flee to the neighbour's garden.

Around 1968 Leonora decided to make some improvements to the house. During the process, she became inspired by the building materials the contractors were using. She began to use cement and iron rods in her sculptures, adding different pigments to create different effects, and, in one instance, designing a completely black effigy by mixing cement with coal. My mother had always had an appetite for detective stories but also got inspiration from tales of real persecution. She and the carpenter devised a secret compartment in her bathroom's double ceiling, to which we had access via an entrance at the top of her walk-in wardrobe. Not just a source of fascination for my son Daniel, who loved that Leonora's house was full of surprises, the compartment also functioned as a necessary hiding place in case government soldiers searched the property. It was also where we concealed our 'weapons', which amounted to a much-used pellet gun and an ancient 30–30 Winchester, unused since the Mexican Revolution, which, if actually fired, would probably have done more damage to its wielder than any assailant. Daniel's dream was to get his hands on this weapon, but it has long since disappeared. On another occasion a friend warned Chiki that the police were going to search the house, so he collected all the substances from my 'chemistry lab' and flushed them down the toilet. The water began to boil, looking for a while as though it might actually explode and shower the entire room with chemicals. Happily, though, the toilet proved to be sturdy, noble and primeval enough to resist this most unlikely of aggressions.

I am reminded again of my political involvements during my university years.

When classes ended for the day, I would head with a group of friends to a café where we sat and talked about all manner of things, not least among them politics and art. One day a group of armed special police burst into the café with their cockroach helmets and anti-riot batons and threw us into one of the sinister police vans known in Mexico as 'Julias'. Some of the girls began to cry, and I tried to calm them down. My fear changed into an ill-advised rage against our captors. At the police station I tried to talk to everyone who crossed my path, even though I was still being shoved along by armed officers. I reasoned that we were being treated brutally and unjustly – I was still relatively naïve when it came to the state's capacity for repression. At the time many young people were considered potential criminals in need of discipline. Hours went by, and eventually Chiki and Leonora came to visit, their frightened faces pleading with me to remain calm. One man wearing a grey suit and red and green striped tie came to give us a speech on good behaviour and morality, but quickly spotted the boredom written all over my face – I find it difficult to hide my emotions. He rearranged his monstrously loud tie, approached me wearing a dirty look, and threatened me with foetid breath: 'Look, you ugly bookworm, if I'm boring you I'll happily throw you into one of our cells instead.' The image of the bookworm was moderately funny – the man noticed my glasses and decided I was a threat, his natural enemy, thereby revealing how much he despised intellectuals. He held power in ignorance. The speech he gave us was peppered with conventional ideas and revealed a veneration for rules and respectability, allow- ing me to judge exactly the kind of background he had come from. I imagine he identified me immediately as his adversary, given the different paths we were forging through the world. My friends and I later learned that we had been denounced by the café owner, who felt insulted by our conversation and had asked law enforcement to intervene. How easy it is to reimagine other people's difference as an offence against the law.

*

The sixties were transformative. It was during this period that the US psychologist and philosopher Timothy Leary came to Mexico. His research into the therapeutic potential of psychedelic drugs had an important impact on the field and contributed to the introduction of psychedelic culture to an entire generation. His experiments with LSD are well documented; they led to his arrest on several occasions and incarceration in a number of US prisons. Mexico's hallucino- genic mushrooms and psilocybin soon caught his attention, and he began to plan the Zihuatanejo Project, a psychedelic training centre and international community based in Zihuatanejo in the state of Guerrero. It was around this time that Leary came to the house on Calle Chihuahua. Leonora had been intent on meeting him in order

to learn some of what he knew about altered states of perception
and meditation techniques. Serge, a French friend and a Leary adept,
left a manual behind after his visit, which I later perused. It refers
to the unlimited realities resulting from the use of LSD, psilocybin,
mezcaline, and other hallucinogens. However, it also noted that
'the experience is not restricted to drug states but can be induced
by (among other things) yoga exercises'. Some of the meditation
exercises it recommended were aimed at sensorial deprivation, and
for this reason the Zihuatanejo Project was interested in *The Tibetan
Book of the Dead*, which was known as an instrument for dealing
with altered states of consciousness and the expansion of consciousness beyond the restraints of the ego.[27] I once asked Leonora's
opinion on this book and the Zihuatanejo Project's decision to base
some of its therapeutic strategies on its teachings. 'Well', she replied,
'they chose this book because they not only aim at self-knowledge,
they also want to work with inner images. The idea was to understand what had occurred during a hallucinogenic trip by following a
Tibetan technique of internal visual stimulation.'

The Tibetan Book of the Dead insists on an initial period of sensorial deprivation where 'there are no visions, no sense of self, no
thoughts', in which one achieves transcendence 'beyond words,
beyond space time, beyond the self'. Leonora, for her part, always
avoided using drug-related stimulants in her pursuit of self-knowledge.
In her opinion, they were full of dangers and not worth the risk.

I remember the day we received several calls from the hospital
in Zihuatanejo. Serge, it transpired, who had been impressed by the
project's work, had become totally immersed in it, taking LSD frequently himself. In his hotel room one night, he was besieged by
nightmarish visions and, unable to bear the assault on his mind,
jumped out of the window. As luck would have it, a large cactus

---

[27] See Timothy Leary, Ralph Metzner and Richard Alpert, 'Tibetan Manual for Ego-
transcendent Experience Using Psychedelic Substances', in *Psychedelic Monograph
No. 2*, 3rd edn (Zihuatanejo, México, 1962; Antigua: I.F.I.T, 1963).

had broken his fall, preventing his otherwise certain death. The victim was merely humiliated; his friends rushed him to a hospital where he had to endure the painful extraction of a large number of thorns from his backside.

In the book he left at our house, Serge had underlined a couple of notes written by Leary and his colleagues Ralph Metzner and Richard Alpert. The three had drawn on Carl Jung's research on *The Tibetan Book of the Dead*, which was understood to be a tool to help us negotiate the phenomenon of death. One such underlined comment from the *Book* referred to the 'disintegration of the wholeness of the Bardo body, which is a kind of "subtle body", constituting the visible envelope of the psychic self in the after-death state'. I can easily see how Leonora might feel an attraction for these forms of interpretation; she was always in search of inner maps to help her navigate her own visionary life and inner demons. When she mentioned Jung's work to me once, I replied that I found his attitude very negative.

'Why do you say that?' she asked.

'Well', I replied, 'among other things I'm not thrilled with the concept of a collective unconscious.'

'What do you have against it?'

'If we agree that there is such a thing as a collective unconscious, shared by every human, without any cultural distinctions, there remains a limited space to acknowledge important dissimilarities between cultural backgrounds and individuals.'

Leonora stroked one of the cats that was snoozing in a pool of sunlight and took a sip of her tequila.

I went on: 'I believe every culture has a unique psychic make-up, so the place where we live and the people we come into contact with influence our unconscious.'

'Can you give me an example?' she asked. In my response, I referred to certain Mexican cultures that recognise a condition called *susto* – a kind of dread or fright. A person affected by *susto* must consult a *curandero* in order to establish what kind of haunted animal provoked the loss of a soul. Research among the Zapotec reported a case of a man who came upon a poisonous snake. Eventually this man consulted a *curandero*; after a while they agreed 'that the encounter with the snake (was the main cause for the *susto*)'.[28] The attack to the subtle body is clear, as these communities believe an immaterial substance, an essence, becomes detached from the body and is vulnerable to supernatural forces. The unwitting offender might disturb 'the spirit guardians of the earth, river, ponds, forests, or collectivities of animals, birds or fish'.[29] These people conceive *susto* as a supernatural illness, and accordingly, they consider that magical circumstances condition the psychic state of the patient.

One of Leonora's most admirable traits was her openness and willingness to listen and question her intellectual preferences.

*

1968 left Mexico deeply wounded, and our family was no exception. The country's political atmosphere pervaded the house. We gathered together a group of people down by Chiki's darkroom, where we used the mimeograph to print anti-government propaganda that left us all covered in stubborn ink stains. The government wanted to clean up for the Olympic Games and decided to repress any political protests. Police and military violence became acceptable in order for Mexico to show how evolved and peaceful it was: a place where nothing but sport and good feelings prevailed. People could no longer gather in large numbers; free expression ceased to exist. We all lived in an atmosphere of fear and indignation against the proto-fascist repressive manoeuvres from the government. This was the situation that culminated with the Tlatelolco massacre.

[28] Arthur J. Rubel et al., 'Description of susto', in *Susto, a Folk Illness* (Berkeley, CA: University of California Press, 1984), p. 34.
[29] Ibid., p. 8.

In reaction to the army's killing of the student demonstrators at Tlatelolco, Leonora asked me to introduce her to some students at the university. Together they planned to march in absolute silence down one of Mexico City's main avenues, dressed entirely in black. They were to set off from the Faculty of Philosophy and Literature. We were to distribute posters around the city – I wrapped the sheaves of paper in a plastic bag and secured them to my torso underneath my shirt. The army had occupied the university, and there were military roadblocks all around it. I was stopped by a soldier as I entered and tried as best I could to remain calm. The soldiers went through my book bag, finding a volume by Stanislavsky and another by Brecht. The sergeant demanded to know who these foreign-sounding authors were, asking whether they belonged to the Communist Party. 'They wrote for and about the theatre', I replied. He let me through, though he looked unconvinced, and as I went past, I tried not to reveal how much my legs were shaking – I could scarcely walk. I have rarely experienced such fear as in those moments. Often, I woke at night to see the soldiers barging into my room and taking me prisoner; fortunately, this was only a nightmare. However, army vehicles patrolled the streets, and I am haunted, too, by a related memory. I was carrying a rucksack full of first aid supplies, approaching the San Carlos Art Academy. Multiple tanks were blocking the street; in one of them, a soldier sat devouring a banana with the same innocence as a monkey in a zoo. The scene took on a comic cast, though with a residual undercurrent of revulsion and fear. Everybody knew that the low-ranking soldiers had been heavily drugged before they opened fire on the group of 'dangerous' students at Tlatelolco.

Before the army's occupation of the university, a lot of political debate had raged in the café of the Faculty of Philosophy and Literature. Students would discuss Che Guevara's ideas and actions, many of them donning versions of his legendary beret. A 'revolutionary' atmosphere took hold, although this didn't prevent the 'comrades' from shouting orders at their female counterparts: to get them a coffee, clean the tables, and be quick about it too. It suited them to play at being revolutionaries. Still, they were simply repeating the same repressive, regressive behaviours they derided elsewhere, oblivious to the fact that treating their female peers in this way was a form of subjugation – the very thing against which they wanted to rebel.

At home, Leonora launched herself headlong into feminist consciousness-raising. We read Simone de Beauvoir followed by Germaine Greer's *The Female Eunuch*, discussing the nuclear family and the tyranny to which women were subjected. Nobody can remain unchanged after reading texts such as these, and Leonora's art grew to take on a much-needed political angle. When climbing the stairs recently, I glanced at an ink drawing of hers that depicts a chained creature, surrounded by unscalable walls, expressing frustration and anger. In it, Leonora alludes to the shameful events of 1968, capturing the moments of anguish we all felt at the effect of state crimes. A couple of years later, Leonora also designed a poster to celebrate the feminist movement in Mexico, which she called 'Mujeres Conciencia', 'Female Awareness', and which we included in an archival exhibition that took place in Biblioteca México (2017) to celebrate her centenary.

Early one morning in 1968, the phone rang. It was a reporter warning that Elena Garro had denounced us to the government. The information was to be released the following day. Leonora risked being detained, and I was also concerned that the police might find the political propaganda we had produced. I had to get rid of it all somehow. Arrangements followed for a new passport so that Leonora and I could flee the country. During this time some intellectuals preferred to keep silent about these repressive events for fear of being detained, and this shocked me deeply. The first available flight out of Mexico was to Chicago, but with the recent assassination of Martin Luther King, the place was experiencing a turmoil all of its own. Leonora was fed up with political upheavals, so we decided to seek sanctuary in New Orleans instead.

I introduced Leonora to Larry Borenstein, who owned a lot of property in the French Quarter there. Some years before, I had met Larry and he offered to lodge me in one of his properties. He led an intriguing life – there were rumours that he was part of the intelligence service, and he was reportedly the grand-nephew of Leon Trotsky. His parents were Ukrainian Jews, and he had worked in circuses and carnivals. He was also hired at the Chicago World's Fair in 1933 as a soothsayer, under the artistic name of 'Prince Cairo'. He later made a fortune as a businessman, buying a great number of properties in New Orleans. Having developed a passion for jazz, he founded Preservation Hall, a venue dedicated to preserving musical tradition and staging jazz sessions. Personalities such as Punch Miller and Kid Thomas performed there on his intimate stage. The building itself dates back to 1800 when it had been a Spanish tavern. Larry told me that police often harassed them; he also mentioned the Noel Rockmore paintings that were inspired by musicians who had performed in his venue. While we were there, I learned to enjoy traditional Dixie, blues, hymns, and rags.[30] The musicians' cheeks would swell as they played their trumpets, their bodies vibrating. It was there that I heard Sweet Emma Barrett for the first time, wearing her red woven skull cap and slamming enthusiastically on the piano keys. These sessions filled me with energy and sheer joy at being alive. Larry, who somehow found the time to collect and sell art, was an admirer of Leonora's work, and thus had offered to let us stay in one of his properties. The heat and humidity of New Orleans, with its nearby swamps, was often exhausting. At nightfall I would walk to Preservation Hall, although Leonora refused to come, being no jazz enthusiast herself. We stayed at a place in the French Quarter, near to which I found an alluring little corner crammed full of plants, where I often enjoyed

[30] See William Carter, *Preservation Hall: Music from the Heart* (London: Cassell, 1991); J. Mark Southern and David Goldfield (eds), *New Orleans on Parade: Tourism and the Transformation of the Crescent City* (Baton Rouge, LA: Louisiana State University Press, 2006).

a cup of coffee and buried myself in John Fowles's *The Magus*.[31] This novel was recommended by my mother and was the subject of much conversation once I had finished it. It didn't take long for me to become completely engrossed in the life of young Oxford graduate Nicholas Urfe, who travels to a Greek island to lecture and makes friends with the enigmatic Maurice Conchis.

Those were, nevertheless, difficult times. I went through many depressive episodes. The unpredictability of our lives back then led to a sort of inner paralysis that would intermittently consume me. I tried to be rid of it as best I could, but every morning was a challenge. I felt so exhausted, as though I were enduring a long convalescence from the recent upheavals in Mexico. They required a period of recuperation, and writing sometimes helped. Friends informed us that Octavio Paz had renounced his diplomatic post as a protest against the Tlatelolco massacre, and this news raised our spirits, leading us to comment on Octavio's courage in the face of such miserable circumstances.

Once the political situation had calmed down, we returned to Mexico, although it was a Mexico that remained in a state of heightened tension. I remember that at the peak of the 1968 movement we had Juan Soriano and one other guest, recently arrived from Italy, come to visit us. One of them, I forget which, narrated a romantic, highly aestheticised scene in which some Italian students wearing flashy clothes confronted the police. Suddenly I could stomach it no more and retorted 'bullshit'. The rest of lunch proceeded in silence. It was pleasant for me, nevertheless, because of where I sat, with the warmth on my back from the clay fireplace that seemed to be straight out of Hieronymus Bosch's *The Garden of Earthly Delights*.

It was hard to keep up with the mosaic of personalities coming through the house on Calle Chihuahua. Leonora at one point befriended a very serious-looking Dutchman who was a spiritual practitioner. The man was corpulent, with a large face, a grave air,

---

[31] John Fowles, *The Magus* (New York: Dell, 1983 [1965]).

and a tendency to blush. Leonora offered to organise a séance, seating our sullen Dutchman and his female friend – frail, black hair, the look of a frightened rabbit – around a small wooden table. They held on to the Ouija board as the Dutchman questioned the spirit. No answer; just silence. He persisted, and this time a timid, supernatural-sounding knocking could be heard. The séance appeared to be a success, and the spirit began to respond with increased enthusiasm. Our man had a feverish look, the black-haired woman dampened her lips nervously, and my mother was visibly outside of herself. She said she thought the spirit belonged to a white stallion, swearing she could see it galloping in the distance. Later that evening, I was startled by a horrible shriek and ran to Leonora's bedroom. The Dutchman was pointing at her with an accusatory finger, the table overturned next to him, his face distorted with anger. This was the order of events: Leonora had concocted a 'spirit machine' by discreetly placing a screw underneath the middle of the table, to which she had attached a nut and a long piece of thread. As Leonora pulled the thread, the nut would hit the underside of the table and emit a haunting sound. Despite multiple invitations issued by a fairly sheepish Leonora, our guests never returned to the house. When I was studying theatre some years later, I came across the 'spirit man' once again. This man invited my whole theatre group to his home, where he gave a very interesting and learned lecture about Brecht. I assume he had, by then, forgotten about the calamitous séance. I, on the other hand, struggled to keep a straight face as I listened to him because scenes of that spiritless spirit session kept coming unbidden to my mind. The demon of merriment accosted me mercilessly.

*

I want to recreate one of those days of intense communication Leonora and I used to have. Ideas came to us like an unstoppable stream, faster than we could express them, each one stumbling over the next. I fumbled for cups of coffee with blind fingers, my ash-tray overflowing with cigarette butts. As soon as Leonora opened her mouth, something else would come to me. We discussed so many things. The latest book we were reading, a new project that we could work on together. We laughed about people who took themselves too seriously. We discussed the time a transwoman visited who tried to hide her hands, to keep her identity safe. I would have liked to say to her: in *this house, you are free to be whoever you choose!* But she remained shy and quiet.

We reminisced about our grey cat called Zephier, much adored, with his beautiful silver coat. Early one morning he brought me a hideous gift as a token of his love. I felt a slight weight on my chest as I was emerging from sleep. I assumed, at first, that it was merely his paw, but then felt something wet and realised something was there. I jumped out of bed when I discovered that his morning offering was a dead mouse. Seeing my expression of horror and disgust, he threw me an indifferent look, convinced not only of my ingratitude but also of my inability to appreciate the finer things in life.

After I graduated, I headed to New York to enrol in a graduate programme at Columbia University. Most of my classes were tedious, and I mainly spent my time drinking tea. Only French literature was interesting enough to keep my attention. I told Leonora how our tutor would gather the group in his living quarters, where a glass box sat on a sturdy table, home to a series of beautiful snakes. 'It sounds like you're more impressed by the reptiles than the subject of the man's lectures', she remarked. She may have had a point. In those classes we seemed to move in and out of the concrete world, with the serpents functioning as a mental escape route (see Plate 10).

Meanwhile, I was looking for an apartment to rent. I became a cat-sitter and plant-waterer when one of Leonora's friends was out of town. I also had Aruk, a lovely-looking chihuahua who was my closest companion, even fitting inside one of my pockets when I went to work at the theatre. In the winter, I had to clean her paws so that the salt on the streets wouldn't burn her skin. At one point, I looked after two salukis belonging to a family that lived in a nineteenth-century brownstone. One of the dogs was called Pulcinella, rebaptised as Dirtynella because she was always filthy. I was glad to eventually find an apartment near the Natural History Museum, a pretty area where there were plenty of good walking routes.

Leonora invited me over for dinner one day when she was feeling very down. A book lay on the table: *Helter Skelter: The True Story of the Manson Murders*, by the prosecutor Vincent Bugliosi, about the terrible murders orchestrated by Charles Manson, who – inspired by a Beatles song – went by the pseudonym Helter Skelter.

'Are you reading this thing?' I asked her.

'Yes, I'm nearly finished with it, you can have it if you want.'

'No, thank you. In fact, I'm going to ask you to throw it away. Reading about murders like that is the sort of thing that can make you sick.'

She agreed fervently and got up to pour our habitual afternoon cup of tea. I tried to express my sense that we have inner bodies that are affected by what we read; these inner bodies can be infected with real poison or nourished by healing encounters. I wanted to talk to her about how we might manage those bodies and her ideas on this matter.

Leonora rinsed our cups and suggested we go for a walk down by Gramercy, a park in downtown New York near where she had lived for quite some time. At one point, she stopped and turned to face me. 'Do you remember Desiderio Lang?' she asked. We used to call him Desi for short, or, more formally, Dr Lang. He was an expert in the Kabbalah. He and Leonora used to get together in the Calle Chihuahua house, sitting around a large travelling case drinking coffee or tequila and talking about the Kabbalistic Tree of Life (see Plate 11). According to Leonora, the Tree could be conceived 'as a cognitive map of Jewish mysticism'. She told me that day that she could still visualise the Tree's symbols, known as *sephiroth*. Lang attributes these to different parts of the body – 'Kether' was the head or brain, and 'Binah' was the heart. Leonora was fascinated by Binah, because, she said, it reminded her of Robert Graves's *White Goddess*. I tried to create a mental image of the *sephiroth* – tradition considers them to be emanations of the divine – because I wanted to learn more about these inner bodies. These symbols seduced Leonora, and she created a lithograph that incorporated them into a

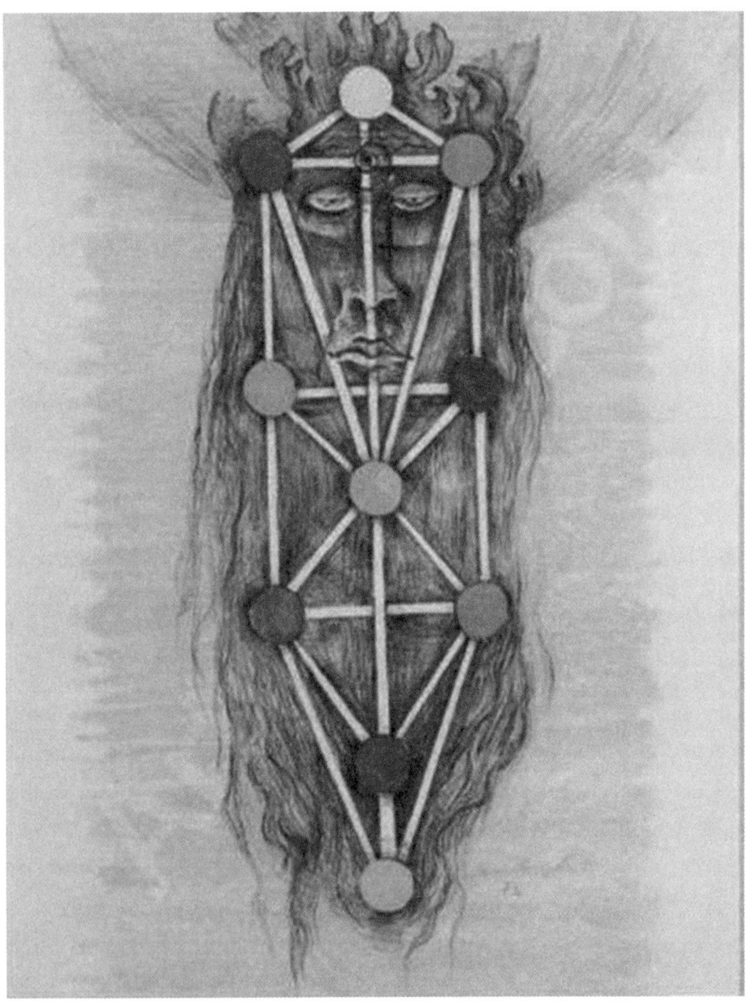

Leonora Carrington, *The Dybbuk*, 1974. Lithograph.

man's face surrounded by the Tree of Life, thus introducing a character of her own as a way of representing the divine.

The depth of my mother's interest in this area was confirmed to me when, recently, I pulled a book from the shelf called *Major Trends in Jewish Mysticism* by the well-known Kabbalah scholar Gershom Scholem.[32] The book was full of notes she had left between the pages, some of which are worth sharing. She wrote:

It's possible that the Kabbalists' complicated numerology was a way of displacing a mental habit in order to open the mind to further possibilities.

I wish I could ask her whether she believed that mental habits prevented us from thinking in other ways. I can practically see her, fishing around in the corners of her mind, wandering down the same confused paths we all traverse from time to time.

It appears that the human psyche secretes a material that is sensitive to impressions not recognised by known reason (patterns).

'Are you implying that there is a part of our thinking structures that can apprehend something our reason cannot?' I want to ask.

This material seems to increase with an emotional stimulus (and of course all the well- known hallucinatory drugs). Rhythm, prayers, etc. increase or evoke activity in this centre of energy.

'I assume', I would have responded, 'that the psyche has a rhythm that emanates from a centre of energy inside us.'

If these impressions were not readily grounded in interpretation according to existing and limited reason, it would be tempting to hope that a new form of a human being might emerge.

These impressions, she seems to be suggesting, which are born out of reason, limit our ability to think and exist. We have a habit of reducing everything to just one level of understanding.

These notes are evidence of the depth of Leonora's reading and ongoing research.[33] That day in Gramercy park, we also talked

---

[32] Gershom Scholem, *Major Trends in Jewish Mysticism* (New York: Schocken, 1954 [1946]).

[33] Personal archive.

about the philosopher George Gurdjieff, who had gathered teachings from Tibet, Iran, India, and the Dervishes.

'Gurdjieff believed', explained Leonora, 'that humans live in a state of permanent stupor or lethargy.' She drew on her cigarette pensively. 'He claimed that human beings resembled machines, and we all had to learn to accept this. Machines are irresponsible; therefore, humans have to learn responsibility.'

'Alejandro Jodorowsky told me that Gurdjieff's father put rats in his [Gurdjieff's] bed when he was very young', I replied.

'What a stupid idea, what did he do that for?'

'From what I understand, it was meant to help him overcome his fear', I replied. My mother's reaction to Alejandro's anecdote shows that her instinct was to question mystification. She challenged the macho tradition of heroism and the narrative of 'great masters', arguing instead that we should learn about our bodies before subjecting them unthinkingly to violence.

I remember that Alejandro asked me over to his house one day, where he pulled out a book and said: 'Read this.' It was an unfinished allegorical novel by René Daumal, *Le Mont Analogue*, about a figurative mountain – an imaginary obstacle – that we must climb if we are to achieve our full potential and inhabit a better world. Daumal, who died in 1944, was a Gurdjieff disciple, and the novel is a fictional elucidation of the different psychic levels his master had elaborated. Leonora became interested in Daumal because *Le Mont Analogue* can be read as a description of different phases of a mental exercise, in which an unconscious body becomes aware of its power as it climbs the mountain. In the novel's pages, readers encounter nebulous places such as those visited by astronauts of the mind such as Nerval, Rimbaud, and Baudelaire in their forays into subliminal landscapes.[34]

---

[34] René Daumal, *Mount Analogue: An Authentic Narrative*, trans. Roger Shattuck (San Francisco: City Lights, 1969 [1952]).

Gurdjieff was like a piece of a mosaic that Leonora was trying to fit into her mind. I remember her coming into the living room in Mexico one time with a book in her hands. 'I've just found something I'd like you to read', she told me. She often behaved as though our whole lives were an ongoing conversation briefly interrupted by the practicalities of day-to-day existence. The book was *Monsieur Gurdjieff*, a leather-bound book by L. Pauwels. The paragraph Leonora wanted me to read was from an interview with Gurdjieff:

> All that you know, all that you call art, is a subjective art, which I would refrain from calling art because I reserve this denomination for objective art [...] Between objective and subjective art, there is a difference. In the first, the artist will acquire a real creation – creating what he intended to carry out, introducing in the work ideas and feelings that he really intended. The effect of his work on people is very precise [...] people receive ideas and feelings that the artist wished to transmit. When dealing with objective art, there is nothing accidental, not the creation of the work, nor the impressions it affords.[35]

I did not entirely agree with what I read in the book Leonora had proffered. I believe art is not always deliberate, nor is it always precise, and nor is the author always willing. Rather, the accidental is often present in art. Leonora responded that what was interesting about Gurdjieff was that, although he was not an artist, he was highly intuitive.

'We are scavengers', I said to her. 'We search for food that is useful for our creative capabilities.'

'I knew you would appreciate the passage', Leonora told me. 'It belongs to our psychic kitchen.'

*

---

[35] George Gurdjieff, 'Notes sur un livre clandestin', in Louis Pauwels (ed.), *Monsieur Gurdjieff: Documents, témoinages, textes et commentaires sur une société initiatique contemporaine* (Paris: Seuil, 1954), p. 96, n. 1.

Back in New York, as she and I walked and talked in the park, we came across a squirrel burying an acorn for safe keeping. It was an image of brevity and beauty that Leonora described as a kind of haiku – the kind of image to which most people are indifferent.

We moved on to discussing different approaches to meditation; Leonora nurtured an interest in underlying worlds. She said to me, 'the Tibetans succeeded in creating artificial shapes which they endowed with an awareness principle that revealed a finite "sensitive existence". Can such shapes be used to convey messages to our consciousness?' When I look at her paintings, as I often do, I see figures and creatures as passageways to intense emotions. Do these shapes modify the viewer's perception? The answer to that question is never clear to me. In some senses, I can see how contemplating them might allow us to visualise the body's psychic centres – to move beyond established mental patterns and perceive other realities. I sometimes wonder if we are all standing before a wall built from our mental habits, a wall that must come down before we can access other realities. I ask Leonora what she thinks. 'We encounter obstacles to knowledge when we obey rules in ways that have become habitual. Mental routine is stultifying because it is unadventurous and lacking in risk.'

I find it difficult to talk about creative agency as though it were something fixed and subject to facile interpretation. But the huge amount of time and effort Leonora invested in understanding herself is easy to identify in her work. She spent hours learning about and practising meditation, and she kept a sketchpad next to her bed that she filled with drawings and notes. 'My paintings don't come exclusively from dreams', she once declared. 'Some scenes emerge from altered states of consciousness. Others – who knows where they come from.' Chatting to her in her studio in Mexico, she explained that the centre of psychic visualisation is the point where the bridge of the nose meets the eyebrows. That is where we locate the meditative image. It is also a screen for the visionary eye, for hypnagogic and dream images. 'You can try it on yourself', she told me.

'Are you saying that one can use meditation techniques as a kind of self-observation method? Can we use them to assemble our narratives, our traditions?' I asked.

'We are only released from our past through acceptance and understanding; the mind is conditioned by the past, by nearly all our experiences and beliefs. Original actions are unique and singular, as in the case of geniuses and heroes.'

'But aren't we all structured by expectations and inventions?'

Leonora paused at this, holding her paintbrush. 'Perhaps', she conceded, 'but there is no excuse for those who reason freely and are therefore free to act without the authority of tradition.'

I thought about what she had said. We construct the past according to what we are taught to fear, according to what we prevent ourselves from being and becoming. I want to avoid being dominated by the authoritarian strictures of our past – our education systems condition us to be obedient and to glorify discipline.

It is windy in New York, and there are a lot of people out in the streets. Leonora holds on to my arm. 'Tradition is the enemy of thought and original ideas', she says. 'One must rid oneself of it and refuse to be its prisoners. It is an incomprehensible and absolute force. Everything becomes possible when ideas become actions – this is the only liberating process we know as humans.' In response to this, I ask, 'Does this mean that when faced with the tyranny of tradition, we can transmute ideas into actions and therefore free ourselves from these restrictions?'

It is a cold day, and at this point we seek somewhere warm to continue our conversation over a comforting cup of tea. We find a table away from the draught where the door opens and closes. Where did we leave off? Leonora asks. We had been discussing the kinds of action that affect our inner lives. My mother takes a sip, savouring the warmth of the tea. 'Wait', she says, 'I'm going to buy her a sandwich.' She is pointing to a bag lady who has stopped to rest her legs. She comes back and we go on with our conversation.

'An act that has been imagined and then executed empowers the psyche because it illustrates what is possible', she says.

'So, that which limits our possibilities is created by our anguish?'

A couple are having an argument in low voices nearby. The exchange is angry, and the man stabs the air in front of the woman's face. Leonora lights a cigarette. 'There is an emotional dynamic, a real motivating force somewhere in our minds. That energy is animated or suppressed by what we think.'

'Maybe the destructive part of the mind can also be creative – perhaps it's an androgynous presence, able to think both ways simultaneously.'

*

I set aside a place in my library for special interest books – texts that evidence Leonora's interest in the Celtic and Irish traditions, alchemy and magic, and even oneiric transmutation. There are many who would impose a mask on her, making her fit their expectations of what a writer should be – especially those who wish to impersonate her. However, there is little point asking how this material may or may not have influenced her work. She never became what she read. She sailed, for instance, through works on Zen and Tibetan Buddhism, but it was all incorporated into her active experience, becoming part of a quest to familiarise herself with any instrument that might help her navigate her inner world. Others saw her as a witch concocting something in an alchemical kitchen. I don't deny that she was interested in alchemy, magic, and many other related subjects. But people tended to overlay their own stories on to her identity.

When I was writing my thesis, Leonora wanted to read the sections on shamanism, associating this material with the Tibetan Bon. 'Let me show you something', she said, proffering a volume.

'This book supports the idea that the Bon was a Tibetan religion before the arrival of Buddhism. They base their teachings on a psyche of the natural, a belief that nature was inhabited by good and evil spirits. It was a shamanistic religion.' I browsed this book again recently and found a note you had written about a sermon of sTon-pa gShenrab's – the founder of the Bon tradition – on the topic of serpents.[36] Reptiles occupied what you acknowledged as a symbolic land for the psyche.

I too had read something about the Bon. 'Little is known about the doctrine because what remains was all written by Buddhists, who aimed to discredit the Bon followers', I told her.

'They were involved in shamanic practices', she offered.

'How so?'

Leonora was scouting about for something for the dog to eat. As she dished him up some food, she elaborated. 'What I mean is that the use of hallucinogens, meditation, and trance states enable awareness.'

I located a text on the Bon, a religion based on 'local god and spirit cults',[37] and as it turned out, my mother was right: I did find these remarks on the shamanic practice of the Bon very interesting. The shamanic tradition 'pertains to practices which communicate with otherworldly beings through alternate states of consciousness'.[38] The shamanic modality 'credited Padma Sambhava with the origins of animal healing'.[39] This understanding of the spiritual world that animals inhabit was central to your feelings about the animal world.

Many of our conversations were about the different ways we might learn about our unseen dimensions. Leonora believed that

---

[36] Samten G. Karmay, 'Introduction', in *The Treasury of Good Sayings: A Tibetan History of Bon* (Oxford: Oxford University Press, 1972), pp. xix, xxii, xxiii.
[37] Claire Hefferman, 'Tibetan Veterinary Medicine', *Nomadic Peoples*, 1.2 (1997), pp. 37–54 (38).
[38] Ibid.
[39] Ibid., section II, 'Animal Healing', p. 43.

'simultaneous scenes pointed to a common psychic place, shared by all beings on this planet'. She imagined real psychic regions, places that could be explored by what she thought of as a visionary body. But she also questioned our forms of perception and the instruments with which we can carry out inner tasks. This work differs from the kind of paid work we're used to, which is nothing more than a way to earn a living. Rather, it teaches us how to be with ourselves as we are because we can alter our habits if we dislike them, or if they make us ill. It helps us acquire the knowledge necessary for us to be present before ourselves, to not lose self-awareness.

I ask myself if I can find any further clues to that self-awareness among what Leonora left in her notes. Seeking them out, I go to a room in my house where we keep all the important documents. Leonora left some yellowing typewritten pages that I keep in large folders.

Leonora realised that society was at a loss for what to do, in the dark about how to learn from our experiences in the unseen dimensions of our selves. I think that the use of drugs and other stimulants can help satisfy our craving to access those dimensions. These are notes about her incursions into the mind:

It is incredible to me that people can get bored when there is so much to explore. All we have to do is close our eyes, and we can enter these regions. We tie all forages to a search for what happens within the self.

Other notes reveal how she strives towards a story, sketching out a narrative environment:

There is a walled garden, a transvestite, Benjie (a little girl), a coconut washer who is transformed into a doll and who has the Listener machine.

Inner narratives are also about journeys, seclusion, transformation into the unknown. In her outlines, Leonora asked herself about 'the unknown', how to represent it, whether it is a physical place, as it appears to be in so many of her paintings. These snippets from her written works are indicators or signposts to be explored, a sounding board for the creation of a personal voice. I continue to gather them: *A deserted city.* A character emerges from stage left, Leonora's mental stage, a character that is *no longer human, an angel.* Leonora begins to probe it, asking how it feels to impersonate this entity. She becomes an explorer of mind-spectres and visions. *What is an angel like? Is it multidimensional? It occasionally wears glasses, is quite hairless, and can become transparent.*

These notes are a wonderful window on to her creative character. As she writes, she brings to life their features and their presence. They are displayed on her inner visionary screen, and therefore materialise in the reader's mind's eye. She was not the only one to struggle with the representation of an angel, of course – think of the biblical Jacob. But in the story she is sketching out here, her angel is a lift attendant. It is not long, either, before we encounter the 'pre-cat-cat', a creature that lives in the liminal zone where what the imaginary creates remains as yet unstable, shapes are unreliable. We can visualise this entity as a cat but it is not quite one; however, this is an entity that has the potential for permanent transformation. Later still, she introduces to the narrative a personified 'mass or crowd'. This crowd lacks individuality; it is unattractive, hostile, and potentially dangerous. Yet in her notes, Leonora stops and asks: *But why, why am I perceived as a horde?* The narrative persona goes on to ask what motivates or triggers each character. Miss B faces her fear of mice; the coconut washer finds the cat; the girl encounters mystery, through Totem and Anti-Totem:

Each of these characters has a Totem (guide), an object or an animal or a plant or a toy. This Totem is the 'soul key' and must be lost and found again in order to open the door to the individual. There they are transformed into the other.

These drafts do not amount to a story as such. Instead, they recount the characters' psyches in a way that might spark a narrative flow. Soon Josephine is introduced, a character with a real passion for messengers, who shapeshifts into a postwoman. All characters remain undefined, in a zone of perpetual becoming. Readers are spectators of miniature stages within Leonora's deep mental recesses. The performances there are complex and humorous, with characters that take the form of mounds of mud, whose identities and behaviour change shape – they are as volatile as visions. They are not finite; their uncertainty is crucial.

The notes move on to talk about a journey:

The Journey. The point where comedy and tragedy end to explore an open tunnel.

Here Leonora seems to be alluding to an expedition free from the passionate uproar and emotional explosiveness of comedy and tragedy. I sense, in these notes of hers, that she built different introspective artefacts for her visionary voyages. She refers to an *auditive machine,* or *listener machine, a black box inside which is lodged a water cylinder connected to a system of tubes.* As toolmakers, we dwell in the impulse to build things, but Leonora likes to play with these visionary machines. She explains further:

Listeners use earphones that connect to a cylinder via a copper tube (like a stethoscope?). The sound is like listening to a conch shell. Hearing is drawn into a void.

It was November 1977, when we were living in New York, when she wrote the following in her diary:

So, I must see through the beloved face. It is a closed door. As they say here on fire exits, 'Keep this door open. It could save your life.' Gaby is trying to observe how the self-machine works. As much as I can see of its wrong computing. (Habits we call them.) Some of them feel 'I want' so destructively.[40]

*

A few years later, my son, Pablito, was born in New York. I was present at his birth – an experience beyond words. I felt a torrent of

---

[40] All previous notes as well as this one belong to my personal archive.

emotions. All my senses were saturated. That explosion of life. My PhD studies were, at the time, very demanding, and I often found myself feeding my son with one hand while holding a book in the other, preparing for our class discussions. I would take a walk around the Natural History Museum park every morning, carrying Pablito, then read another book and take notes.

I spent a couple of months in Mexico before heading back to New York, where my daughter, Aggie, was soon born. I went through the same experiences I'd had with Pablito, as though they were some sort of initiation ritual. Leonora looked after Pablito while I rushed to the hospital. It was Halloween and the kids who lived in our building were knocking on doors asking for treats, dressed up in the latest terrifying disguise, all bought from the same costume shops. When Pablito opened the door and saw the grotesque masks, he started to panic. Leonora had to calm him down, explaining that they were just other children wearing masks, that all those monsters and all that blood – none of it was real. She asked one of the boys if he could remove his mask to show him. Pablito hid behind his grandmother as the boy smiled, both proud and a bit sheepish, and took off his disguise. He could scarcely hide his pleasure at having successfully frightened someone.

One evening I received an anguished phone call from Leonora and quickly got on the subway to visit her. I discovered that she'd been found wandering, completely disoriented, through the Holland Tunnel – a major thoroughfare running under the Hudson River that is extremely dangerous for pedestrians. It was clear to me that she was going through a crisis of some kind. It corroded her. She barely acknowledged my presence, remaining unresponsive when I spoke to her. Frankly, I was alarmed. She had been spending time at a Buddhist retreat where she had rationed her meals and subjected herself to excessively rigorous training. I asked her to draw an animal.

'I don't feel like it.'

'Please, trust me, just try.'

It took a lot of cajoling before she finally agreed, moving sluggishly, and managed to draw a cat. I decided to stay with her until she seemed more like her old self. I gave her some relaxation exercises to do and made her a cup of herbal tea. It was a couple of hours before her paleness subsided, and she began to recognise her surroundings once more.

I suppose I should have expected this sort of thing. Individuals who have a passion for exploring their inner worlds are exposed to a certain amount of violence. The hidden life is not devoid of risks. The pursuit of self-knowledge combined with a permanent curiosity – that was Leonora's force, her source of experimentation, her means of survival. People who tried to understand her always found explanations for the way she was; I can still hear my father saying: '*Elle est angoisée*, she suffers from anxiety', or 'she is terrified'. Sometimes the diagnoses were even more extreme, as when she was pronounced incurably insane by the fascist Spanish doctors in Santander. Exploring the unknown parts of the mind has its perils because the 'otherness' of our self might be unpleasant and difficult to manage. Quick psychiatric interpretations fall short of appreciating the nature of that otherness.

When having dinner with a friend once in New York, Leonora wondered aloud how we might define magic. 'Magical thought', she said, 'is something conscious, an impartial search for inner space.' Our host had poured some excellent wine, which we enjoyed as we talked. The host replied, 'Those kinds of spaces are fascinating.' I suddenly felt I had to express something. 'Of course they are, but one can have very daunting encounters there. They are not comfortable or safe spaces.' Leonora petted our host's enormous Russian blue and picked up where she left off. 'You have to discover yourself there, abandon known rules and consider the consequences. Each person has to do this for themselves.' Like explorers from previous times who launched themselves into uncharted territory, you have to unfold a subjective map and scrutinise it to figure out where to begin your search.

In my personal archive I recently found some of Leonora's notes on the question of the magical body:

But what is the point of these queries? I can't seem to find any grand answer, because each person has to find their own. This is the clue to all magic, and it is always excluded from all instructions on magical practice.

The notes go on to guide us through the process of transfiguration into the animated vision of an animal. *Choose different animals, horned, winged, felines or canines, assume their essential flesh as a whole.* I can sense Leonora's enthusiasm in these lines as she animates an imagined body, observing *the way it moves.* She proceeds with this invocation:

Even someone as stupid as to believe in primary solids intuits that these creatures are still alive and in perfect health after a total conversion. Pull the whole skin over yourself by the soles of your feet.

Leonora knew that these manoeuvres involved different phases:

At first, this process should be practised with long strips from the animal's skin – like a bandage – which ought to be unwrapped in inverse spirals from the soles of the feet to a few inches over the head.

If only I could talk to Leonora now as I once could. I want to ask her if those forms belong to a repertoire of skills from our visionary bodies, whether they are shapes that require the transmigration to mental shores where we would gain an imaginary 'awareness' of how to shape or be moulded by our chosen animal. Her notes continue thus:

If you believe that what I said is metaphorical, you must realise that you are condemned to absolute failure. When the skin has been attached permanently, the evidence is that you can cross through dreams, the volatile elements can be contained safely in the all.

I imagine her sitting nearby, slowly and quietly taking on the visionary body. It appears like a living sculpture shaped in her inner dimension. I see her pull a cigarette out of the pack, adjust a filter to the hookah, light the cigarette and inhale deeply before resuming. *This exceptional practice allows you to dance like the sidhe, jump like a flea, run like an antelope and fly like a bird all night.* The *sidhe*, she explained to me some time ago, were creatures that appeared in Irish lore hovering over the surface of the earth. She finishes her notes with the following:

Do you understand the teachings of this essential practice? Do you know what it means to come armed with all the hockma beasts?

The *hockma*, Leonora explained to me once when we read about the Kabbalah, was *the Hebraic version of Sophia or knowledge.* She pointed at her bookshelf and I pulled down a thick black book. We read in these rabbinical texts how Angel Uriel took on the shape of a lion.[41] The sibylline beings Leonora describes in her notes draw both on these and Celtic texts; she combined animal skins with psychic visualisations in order to bring them to life. Regarding the Tree of Life, I found something that could interest Leonora. This has to do with Asherah, who was worshipped in ancient Israel and was both a sacred object and a goddess – according to the biblical scholar P. K. McCarter she was 'a wooden cult object'.[42] We learn that she was a pre-biblical Canaanite goddess connected with the Tree of Life. Another manifestation of this fascinating deity is found in the south-west of England. 'She is represented as standing on a lion; above her a disk and a crescent – perhaps the sun and moon. She is almost naked and is holding a lotus blossom and serpents.'[43]

I want to understand how Leonora shaped these visualisations in her narratives and paintings. I discovered among her writings the story of a young woman who wanted to take on the form of a hyena to avoid the embarrassment and suffering of a debutante ball, an English social ritual in which marriageable young women were presented to society – one which Leonora herself had had to

---

[41] See I. Abrahams and C. G. Montefiore, *The Jewish Quarterly Review*, XI (New York: Macmillan, 1899), p. 17.

[42] J. A. Emerton, 'Yahweh and his Asherah: the Goddess or her Symbol?', *Vetus Testamentum*, 49.3 (1999), pp. 315–37 (317).

[43] Asphodel P. Long, 'Asherah, the Tree of Life and the Menorah: Continuity of a Goddess Symbol in Judaism?', The First Sophia Fellowship Feminist Theology Lecture, College of St Mark & St John, Plymouth, 4 December 1996, p. 5.

endure in her youth. In the story, the hyena reveals to the debutante that in order to take her place, she must take on a human appearance. She plans, therefore, to rip off the face of someone in the woman's household. I shy away from making a too-easy association between this story and Leonora's other notes on transfiguration – interpretation is always a suspicious artifice. After all, the connection might be nothing more than a happy coincidence.

In *The Inn of the Dawn Horse*, Leonora's self-portrait from 1934 (see Plate 12), when King George V was on the throne, she appears sitting in a chair in a room, looking out at the viewer. Her right arm points to a hyena, which also looks out in a disturbing way, as though it means to haunt us, to become our animal spirit-guide. This self-portrait seems to suggest a possible setting for the debutante story; its composition might provide a narrative background.

In a photograph in the family album, Leonora appears in an elegant white debutante dress. My grandmother stands beside her. She was to be presented at court like all the other aristocratic ladies. She looks impassive here, but in 'Debutante', the story, she sends the hyena in her place. The painting and the story were, perhaps, used to perform a psychic exorcism of that English initiation ritual.

A few years ago, Paty and I were at the Metropolitan Museum while a workshop for people with dementia and Alzheimer's was going on. The workshop was an opportunity for these people to interact with the museum's artwork. Paty informed the workshop leader that I was Leonora Carrington's son and that if they wanted, we could work with them on *The Inn of the Dawn Horse*, which is on display there along with a series of other Surrealist works. A vague sense of panic overtook me when we reached the portrait and the workshop leader gestured to me to go ahead. I took on a storyteller's persona, talking to the visitors about Leonora's love for animals and her special devotion to horses and hyenas. I began to feel a special bond with this audience, and I realised that I ought to get them to participate. 'What do you feel when you look at this portrait?' I asked. I was delighted by their enthusiasm and interesting questions. I could sense their enjoyment as if they were surfacing lethargically from an underworld where they had been denied the right to exist outside of their clinical diagnoses. The team that worked with these people in the museum was fully aware that interaction with art was crucial for them. I, too, knew that participation, games, and an active imagination are all fundamental healers. At this juncture, I improvised a story about the portrait, and the role played by the hyena in Leonora's narrative. We all then pitched in for some roleplay involving each of the characters and objects seen in *The Inn of the Dawn Horse*. The painting is a window into a fictional world that has to be activated. If we succeed in unveiling our own personal animal – a hyena, a horse, or whatever creature it might be – then we are in touch with our main source of an inner life.

I remember being in Leonora's bedroom when she was reading to me from a book called *Dreambody: The Body's Role in Revealing the Self* by Arnold Mindell:

Understanding and accepting the Dreambody as a process [...] requires factual knowledge about its behaviour and the courage to go to one's own limits in order to let the Dreambody come into awareness. For the Dreambody hovers between bodily sensation and mythical visualisation.[44]

'What is it that's so compelling about these visions?' I asked Leonora. She replied, 'I assume Mindell is referring to those archetypes that underlie mythical visualisations.' Looking back, it is clear to me that she was engaging with animals and the exchange of bodies and nature in her Dreambody paintings, which allowed her to achieve transformation. Art is the transformative stuff of inner bodies. Black humour always arrives unannounced in her work, making it more

---

[44] Arnold Mindell, 'The Dreambody', in *Dreambody: The Body's Role in Revealing the Self*, ed. Sisa Sternback, Scott and Becky Goodman, intro. Marie-Louise von Franz (Santa Monica, CA: Sigo Press, 1982), p. 8.

effective – it has the power to wake up the savage part of us, our inherent beast that flees domestication despite our schooling and the way society encourages us to despise and distrust this part of our nature.

Leonora was often inspired by animal skins. This became a recurrent theme in her work and was often associated with transformations. You can see it, for instance, in Thibaut, the protagonist of her story 'Monsieur Cyril de Guindre', who had 'a golden skin like the corpse of an infant preserved in an old and excellent liqueur'.[45] You can also see it in 'Pigeon, Fly!', in which the narrator describes the people around her: 'The laughter sounded like bleating sheep, and looking around me, I had the vivid impression I was surrounded by a flock of bizarre sheep dressed for a gloomy ritual.'[46] These lines make me think of the lambs' bleating that caused my mother so much pain on her terrible trip to Portugal accompanied by the sinister Frau Asegurado. The fissures in her disguised characters allow me to glimpse the cracks in daily life, its decomposition. They reveal unvisited territories, like those traversed by Alice, Lewis Carroll's character who made it through the looking glass, and who Leonora so admired. She once told me that 'most of our minds are asleep; lacking activity, they will get sick and begin to die, eventually reaching a state of absolute normality'. Characters such as Alice, on the other hand, nourish our creative minds.

I came across another section in Leonora's 'Pigeon, Fly!', this time with a protagonist who is in some ways her mirror image. The character is a female painter who has the task of painting a portrait of a female corpse that has already begun to decompose. I wonder whether this story was born out of my mother's visit to the land of death, as she understood it in her personal mythology. The story includes a very visually compelling scene in which the dead

[45] Leonora Carrington, 'Monsieur Cyril de Guindre', in *The Seventh Horse and Other Tales*, p. 34.
[46] Leonora Carrington, 'Pigeon, Fly!', in *The Seventh Horse and Other Tales*, p. 23.

woman emits an intense radiance. But no sooner does the painter-protagonist step back to consider her work than she discovers that she has painted her own portrait. Leonora is telling her story here, inhabiting her narrative. There is a mirroring effect at work, in which she uses her double to convey something specific about herself. In the story, a letter addressed to 'Eleanor' is found, in which the writer reveals that she suffered from such extensive loneliness that she was forced to speak to her own image in the mirror. She also describes her husband as being dressed in white feathers, his body phosphorescent, emitting an intense radiance just like the body of his wife. Terrified that she was going to vanish, she tried to paint herself, but could not because her body was already disappearing. To try to stop this process, she took on a disguise, acquiring a flesh of sorts in order to avoid dematerialisation. There are, therefore, two narratives of skin here – while the husband morphs into a white dove, the dead wife masks herself in another's skin to avoid her evanescence. The story ends with a narrative sleight of hand when Eleanor realises that the portrait has vanished. Leonora experimented with matter, it is clear, not only in her visual art but in her narrative art, too.

Some of her emulators have wanted to impose a particular identity on her work, claiming that Mexican culture had a definitive influence on her. They talk about art as though it was wrapped in cellophane, with all its parts visible. Let me sketch out the kind of environment Leonora was working in when she first came to Mexico City. It is true that Mexico attracted artists from all over the world. Trotsky and André Breton wrote a manifesto called 'Pour un art révolutionnaire indépendent' (Towards a Free Revolutionary Art) in 1938; Trotsky did not sign it, but Breton and Diego Rivera did, and thus the Federation of Revolutionary Artists was born.[47]

[47] Figura Starr, 'Diego Rivera's "The Communicating Vessels"', *Print Quarterly*, 13.4 (1996), pp. 413–15 (415).

Mexico City was a singular mixture of politics and art, out of which was born a Surrealism that aimed at absolute creative liberty. It positioned itself in direct opposition to Stalinism, a regime that repressed people, ideas, and art. The authors of the manifesto positioned themselves, too, in opposition to Hitler's regime. It is possible that these circumstances attracted other Surrealist artists to Mexico, in search of an atmosphere of political and creative liberty.

Leonora did not adhere to any specific political ideology; rather, her politics were a direct opposition to injustice. Her life was a long struggle to achieve liberty as a woman and as a painter. Her feminism was therefore very personal, opposing the bourgeois English institutionalism that had threatened to deform her childhood and adolescence. Hers was a politics of self, quite different from the oft-invoked masculine repertoire of muses, femmes-enfants, and eroticism that appears in so much other Surrealist artwork as a way of expressing strangeness. My mother rebelled against these metaphors for female otherness.

A problem arises regarding whether I can depict Leonora's subjective experiences in Mexico, however; are we experiencing her 'real' inner life, or does this belong to a narrative persona. Again, I look through different writings and fortunately I come across some of her notes. One of her narrators describes a Mexican village on a festive day at the marketplace; it gives us a useful insight into the impact that her surroundings had on her imagination:

Every few minutes a rocket goes up and pops loudly in the grey sky. The other band, Rancheros, now starts playing La Texana, Hierba Mala – Bad Weed. Around the Town Hall, they call The Palace are clusters of bright colours, balloons, spun sugar and large toys to win at the games – panthers, dogs, pink Buddhas with pendulous tits [how did he get here?], *bright pink spotted gorillas, morose blue-eyed eagles and Cantinflas* [a comedian]. *Then all the festive food, totopos* [fried tortillas], *tostadas* [fried tortillas with cheese and beans], *fancy bread, pambazo* [bread dipped in red salsa], *fruit, cazuelas* [bowls] *full of red and green salsas. Stalls selling eatables of every kind.*

Everyone is excited about the parade, even police cars are poshed up for the occasion. 'Tonight, there will be fireworks,' says an old woman with a child. 'They go on celebrating till midnight.'

Leonora's photographic memory registers every detail. *The volcanoes were visible from here when we first arrived, through the clean air. They were snow covered. It was different then. This was a separate village, now it's part of the city.*

Leonora's character, an extension of herself, then has a change of mood, becoming *apprehensive as she approached the house.* The narrator's movements reveal this tension, this invisible but powerful state of mind whose cause is undefined:

She went upstairs cautiously, to her room. But this is a game I'm playing Bogey Man. Coward and fool. Stop this. Ah, the enemy within me telling me. But it is a game. I would like it to stop. I must get out, go away. But where?

How many times did we talk about this enemy occupying our inner stage, one that visits at dawn and releases its venom, a poisonous creature that feeds on our negative emotions. Leonora resumes:

Mae thought she didn't dare watch the fireworks in the plaza after all. She served herself a tequila from the bottle she hid behind several stout volumes of natural history – she enjoyed drinking alone, now, in secret – somehow feeling accompanied. This must be old age, she thought.

Leonora projected herself on to an old body, living, acting out, feeling that moment. I have selected these paragraphs as a response to those who have stated so directly that she absorbed Mexican culture. She lived it intently, her complex voice manifesting all those mood changes, displaying an incredible ability to observe and depict this festive environment that the character Mae found herself, for some reason, unable to join.

I'm overcome with nostalgia as I look at the photo album that takes me back to the little house we owned in Cuernavaca. We would sit at the table on the front veranda drinking tequila or a Bloody Mary, the spirits warming the throat as they slipped down. The jasmine plants scented the air deliciously. A humming-bird would flit down to hover over the flowers like an apparition. Sometimes we would talk, but often we shared an enjoyable silence, the dogs chasing each other round the garden. We would find the occasional scorpion crawling around, a visitor from the Ordovician period, ancient and noble. We respected them.

I think back to all those trips we took through little villages, the sun touching our faces like carnival masks in some pagan ritual. There would always be an itinerant performance taking place not far away. I understand so well the feelings Leonora attributed to Mae in her story. The domain of the marvellous is always among us. There are stalls just like the ones in the San Cristóbal of her tale, selling delicately designed *rebozos* or fruit that lies in wait like a still life. A man stretches out a white sheet of dough between two sticks, an expert juggler. He looks to me like a large praying mantis catching an insect in its front legs. He extends the floury sheet and lays it skilfully in a large pan full of bubbling oil – this is how we make a *buñuelo*.

As we walk to another section of the market a man opens a suitcase, a Pandora's box from which he extracts a set of old photographs showing deformed women, victims of terrible diseases, a repulsive nest of worms squirming as they feed enthusiastically on a wound. The quack doctor makes an elegant bow and pulls out a serpent, tame as a cat, that allows itself to be manipulated by him. 'Ladies and gentlemen do not suppose me to be a snake vendor. I do not sell these creatures. But listen carefully – if you ever come across a serpent, do not kill it. Many people believe they are creatures of the devil, but it is not so. Never kill a snake; snakes are money.' The man strikes a dramatic pose. 'The other day, one woman screamed that I was ready to kill a snake and force her to eat it. Not so, ladies and gentlemen.' At this point, he approaches us. 'Have you ever eaten snake? No? You do, though, I suppose, eat other filth like pork. I have tried everything, and now I only feed on serpent flesh.

I assure you' – at this moment, he points to the photographs laid out on the ground – 'that it can prevent all these illnesses.' He takes his time, allowing everyone a glimpse of the photographs. 'You probably expect me to kill one of my snakes. That I will never do.' He handles a snake, which gently slithers up his arm. Men, women, and children alike observe the performance with a mixture of revulsion and fascination. One of the reptiles approaches a pile of rubbish and flicks her forked tongue sweetly.

We move on to where a nearby vendor is displaying papier mâché masks with impressive twisted horns and bright colours that shine through their varnished surfaces. A festive atmosphere takes hold of the place, the noise of wooden rattles surrounding us as though the gods were cracking their bones. Inside the church, the pale and sickly faces of virgins and saints in full regalia look down with melodramatic expressions from beside the altar where people gather. 'I sell serpents!' screams the quack doctor. His female assistant throws him a mocking look. The popular street theatre of the remedy vendor. The sun paints shadows on faces and stalls. A man in elegant white trousers announces that he has 'Chinese fans for sale!' Most of the time we keep our silence, our senses captivated by the mosaic of aromas – copal incense, food – and sounds – laughter, the selling of merchandise, all the indescribable things that belong in the street on market day.

I once described to Leonora a trip I'd taken with my family to Michoacán. There, landscapes stretch like desiccated iguanas shedding their tiny scales in a witches' market. The desert colonises everything, leaving only little shrubs, and occasionally a grove of jacarandas, those majestic trees with their subtle colouring that makes them look like Japanese prints, vanishing as soon as they are looked at directly. Sometimes the purple groves are swapped for flaming red Tabachin trees. We are heading for the Camécuaro lake, which is surrounded by Ahuehuete trees – Moctezuma cypresses. There is something about the bark and little leaves on these giants that fills me with happiness. I sense that this is something Leonora and I would enjoy together, so I try to describe the scene to her as best I can. The place is exceptional. There is crystal clear water dotted with little moss islands that travel like lake creatures through unknown worlds. It is unfortunate that other humans are impervious to the place's delicate beauty, bringing portable radios that insult the quiet. But I suppose we all enjoy places in our own way. Some visitors leave empty cans; others throw paper and other rubbish into the lake. We walk along the shore and encounter some youngsters selling river prawns.

Further on, a group of people gather around an old woman heating tortillas over a *comal*, a metal griddle. When she spots us, she puts on an aggressive, sarcastic English accent, screwing up her face and imitating Paty, Pablito, and Aggie, all of whom are blonde. She sprays us with her rage as she strikes a pose, revealing a pair of dirty legs covered in painful-looking sores. Her skin suffers. She does not scare me, but she makes me sad. Perhaps I am assuming too much about her, however. She lives in a place that is unknowable to me.

Like a vision, a mare with two foals emerge from a field. They canter around elegantly, frolicking together. When we pass through a hillside town, there is a woman dressed in a beautiful embroidered blouse with large crimson flowers on it and a blue and black striped *rebozo*. Paty admires her attire. 'I'll sell it to you', the woman offers, pointing at her clothing. 'No, thank you, that blouse wouldn't look half as good on me as it does on you', Paty replies. The red earth stands in contrast to the svelte adobe houses with their dark tiles. We head on to a place called Ixtlán de los Hervores where there is a geyser. An impressive column of water several feet high bursts from the ground. Pablito and Aggie are thrilled with the idea that we can cook an egg over the boiling water jetting up from a crack in the rock. People are bathing in the steaming water. A few mesquite plants grow nearby, lifting their blanched limbs like supplicant spirits, their branches gnawed by the sulphurous steam.

The gushing water is impressive, like a huge hissing snake. The crust of the earth seems so thin here. Only a few metres down the temperature is infinitely higher – I can feel its intensity through the soles of my shoes. A veil of steam spreads outwards, hovering several feet above the ground. This antediluvian *mise en scène* demands silence. I am overcome by a peculiar lethargy; all communication stalls in the presence of this ebullient giant bursting from its prison in the bowels of the earth. I am overwhelmed with anguish, as though my innards are echoing the smouldering of the earth's viscera, an earth that was once the ancient spectator of colossal dinosaur battles.

It was on that same trip that we had to collect some money for friends. Our hostess led us into a living room furnished with large velvet sofas and rows of shelves displaying porcelain figures. As I took it all in, I remembered how Leonora and I used to call such objects *conneries bourgeoises*, bourgeois stupidities. These obscene items were impervious to our critical gaze, unabashedly flaunting their cuteness. My children ran around and shoved each other, playing boisterously, their limbs flailing dangerously close to the porcelain figures. It was a catastrophe waiting to happen. Our hostess began by bragging about her progeny's financial success before moving on to reveal, in a much more subdued tone, some of their professional mishaps. She declared that times were difficult for their family, though judging by the abundance of useless and expensive knick-knacks around the house, I doubted it. Pablo interrupted her to ask about the money we had come to collect, saying, 'I want to leave.' His words echoed my alter ego's desire to escape the place. Adult conversations habitually hide the complex rituals of social animals. Aggie and Pablito, however, shoved each other playfully, deep in the porcelain forest. They grazed the delicate fake flowers that decorated the table and wrestled each other with diabolical gusto. The objects trembled as if communicating their fear of annihilation. Our hostess poured me a cup of dreadfully strong coffee that made my nerves dance. Tradition, it seems, demands that males be rewarded with an intense beverage equivalent to their perceived level of virility. Paty had better luck than I; she enjoyed a daintier, less aggressive cup of coffee. In an act of accidental violence, I upset my cup over the immaculate white tablecloth embroidered with intricate patterns. The profane brew left a black stain on the pristine white surface. My hostess was quick to apologise for my clumsiness, insisting that this disaster was nothing. Still, I could tell from her body language that she was fantasising about a violent murder. I pictured myself hanging from her chandelier, red tongue lolling. She asked us to stay for dinner, nonetheless – Paty and I promptly declined. Still, Pablito and Aggie were ravenous after their exploits and, far from bashful, eagerly accepted the offer of food. They slurped happily on their milk and chocolate. As the good woman began to complain about the shortage of milk and the shocking price of chocolate, my children, on cue, asked for second servings of both. The woman eventually exited and came back carrying a thick envelope. She suggested I count the money, and so I stepped reluctantly into the legendary world of dollars, counting and recounting for what seemed like an eternity. Meanwhile, the children were behaving progressively worse – I am sure they could sniff out my anxiety.

The Michoacán trip overall was a good one. We had been hungry for indefinable experiences and returned feeling satisfied. It is impossible to speak of absolutes because our experience is the sum of all contrasts. Humans live through things – fictions, on the other hand, imagine flawlessness and dramatise imperfections. Nonetheless, we had felt, as we travelled through the state's shamefully poor towns, a deep wounding of the senses.

Another excursion with the kids took us to Taxco, where houses sprout up all over the mountainside, making the place look like a Tower of Babel. As I recount the trip to Leonora, I admit that we had a dreadful night there. On one side there was a rowdy couple arguing and on the other a woman laughing like a hyena while her male counterpart snorted heavily. After a hearty breakfast the next morning we visited one of the silver shops for which the town is famous.

Later Pablito and Aggie play in the pool with some teenagers they have befriended. A courting ritual ensues, in which the boys carry out risky, heroic stunts and the girls encourage them, laughing shrilly. They remind me of a flock of birds, complete with songs and mating rituals. There is a certain indifference on the part of the girls – their inaccessibility makes them all the more desirable. This poolside courtship ritual follows its natural course, the muscular males displaying their bodies, the *belles dames* looking absent and indifferent, pretending to prefer private, secret conversations. What is peculiar is the firm distance the boys and girls keep from each other, like prey and predators who periodically switch roles. Another part of the swimming pool is taken up by a group of American girls who watch Aggie and Pablito as they splash around and play. Another kind of courtship ritual entirely plays out between these two groups, expressed via envious, scoffing exclamations. The girls point at my children: 'They're crocodiles! There goes one crocodile, there goes another.' I am thrilled when Aggie turns to them and responds, 'If we're crocodiles, then all of you are snakes.' The girls take off, giggling with embarrassment, not having expected Aggie to understand their English. I am delighted with my daughter's ability to stand her ground, noticing how her character is developing.

A couple of years later, a heavily pregnant Paty gets up in the night and tells me we have to head to the hospital. They have closed one of the roads for construction work, and my anxiety rises as I try to find an alternative route. When we eventually arrive, a nurse hands us each a gown to put on. Paty hasn't had any contractions yet, but her waters have broken. I remember Aggie and Pablito's births now that the doctor insists Paty should take an anaesthetic. He had a hard look, with little trace of intelligence, and ruled out any discussion; his word was law. The law, however, was not obeyed – Paty did not want to miss out on her own birth experience. This time, again, she tries to relax, the heavy hand of an intern applying pressure to her stomach like a stone sphinx. Through the window there is a timid splash of light across the sky. Dawn loses its dark skin, fog embraces the buildings, making them vanish like a conjuring trick, and an uncertain light begins to cloak the mountains.

There is an unexpected change of venue. Before we know it, Paty's bed is in the delivery room. It is only a matter of hours before Danny enters the world, abandoning the human cavity where he had been living as an aquatic animal. He is whisked away by the doctors who want to run some tests. It is over, and I am dead tired, though my efforts are nothing compared to what Paty has undertaken. Another long hike, I say to Leonora, like Pablito's and Aggie's births. I ask her if she remembers telling me about my birth at the Hospital de Beneficencia Española, the Spanish Welfare Hospital. She was short on money, so somebody lent her a bedsheet – that was how she and Chiki brought me home, wrapped up in a sheet.

After Danny's birth, I had to go outside for a smoke. Tears poured out of me as though they belonged to another person. The paediatrician eventually led me to Danny's crib, where tubes protruded from his body like translucent serpents. The doctor adopted a wise, Confucian pose, and delivered his verdict: 'Premature babies have no word of honour.' He revealed that Danny had a respiratory defect. As a result, Paty was allowed to go home, but Danny remained in intensive care. We had to don a mask and gown every time we visited. His tiny body struggled with all the tubes emerging from it; they covered his head with an oxygen hood. Those were tense, sad hours. Every time we returned to the house our anxiety would rise, whispering in our ears. We were only allowed five minutes each with him at a time. The head nurse in the intensive care unit was like an impressive termite queen, ruling despotically over her white, metallic domain. The place was an enormous dairy, where multiple women had milk suctioned from their breasts to feed the infants. Everything was subject to a series of inflexible rules. We felt as though Danny had come to belong to the institution, and we had no say in his care. As we know, rules always turn out to be a kind of simulation – I caught a doctor leisurely pulling out a cigarette despite being in a restricted area where there were numerous 'no smoking' signs.

After ten long days, they released Danny from the hospital. For the first time, we were able to bring him home and enjoy being with him. Pablito and Aggie became his loving guardians. Leonora's bond with Danny was strong, too; they had character traits in common, making them part of the same guild. They would have private conversations in a secret language of their own. Danny has Leonora's acute ability to read people. In short, they knew how to be with one another. Danny worked with ceramics at school, where they had a small kiln. The teachers fired a couple of his pieces after he applied a glaze, and he gave the best ones to Leonora, who cherished them. Do you recall, Leonora, when Danny was quite small, he looked out of the window to see a hummingbird feeding? The cat, too, had spotted the bird and was grinding her teeth intently. Noticing, Danny scolded her thus: 'Hey! Vanessa! Stop bothering that hummingbird, or it's going to catch AIDS!'

*

I want to describe some of the work Leonora and I did together, but first there's another piece of art that needs describing: a beautiful, round, blue-glazed ceramic bowl that stood on a desk in our house. On one side there was an engraving of a fish gently swimming through its sapphire dominion. On the other was a hybrid creature, half-bird, half-human, the body made of four intersecting petal shapes. A hirsute ape ran between the two, holding a thin feather. The figures seemed to be in a diorama of sorts. The inside of the bowl was a delicate salmon colour. Leonora had made it with Helena Lincoln, a friend of hers who introduced her to the art of ceramics. Unfortunately, Leonora was never able to continue this kind of work because, by that time, the wet clay made her finger joints hurt.

On the wall in my house hangs a gift from Leonora, which never ceases to amuse me. She gave it to me when I was about to receive my master's degree in English literature. She was struck by an idea and purchased a piece of parchment on which she painted a majestic insect-man and captioned it 'For Master Dragonfly' (see Plate 10). She had turned me into a humanoid insect. I hope my destiny is not the same as that of Kafka's legendary character. No other degree certificate is to be found hanging on our walls, but this one will always have pride of place. It is far more interesting than any other I received from the university. What's more, it acts as a permanent reminder not to take myself too seriously.

The Dark Book was one of many different collaborations between my mother and me. It combined her extraordinary etchings with a

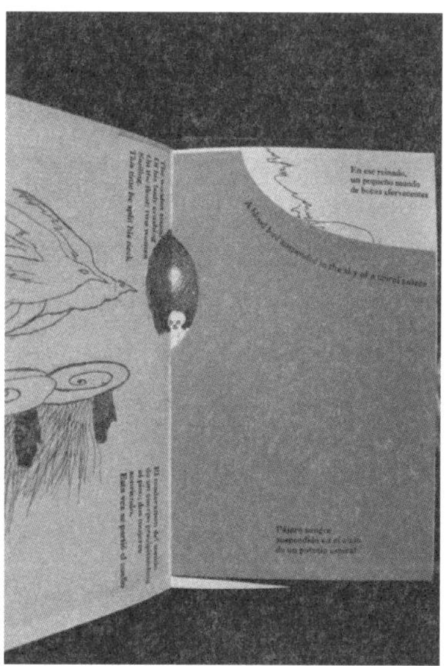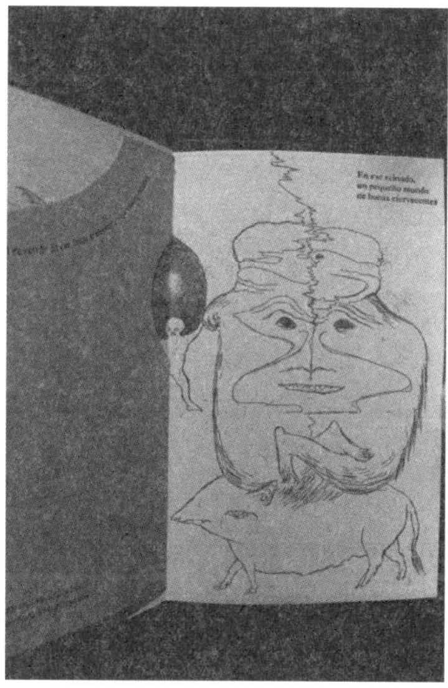

Leonora Carrington and Gabriel Weisz, *Dark Book*, 1996. Etchings, aquatint and texts, 25 × 16 cm. © 2020 Estate of Leonora Carrington / Artists Rights Society (ARS), New York.

series of my poems.[48] It is a *livre objet* reminiscent of those children's books with figures hidden under flaps and windows that open on to discoveries. Etchings inspire poems and poems inspire etchings. The editor suggested that the images might be sold separately so that buyers could hang them on their walls. Still, Leonora and I insisted that the purpose of the *livre objet* was to encourage dialogue between image and text and that they should, therefore, be bound together. It is a playful book that sparks the visual and narrative imagination; they printed only sixty copies. On the day it was presented at the Galería de Arte Mexicano, I came up with the idea of blowing up a few pages from the book and hanging them from the ceiling as a kind of mobile. Years later, we organised another presentation at the Brewster Gallery in New York, where I read a couple of pages from the book.

In the years that followed, we initiated a series of sculpture projects, most of which developed out of one of Leonora's paintings. She planned each one scrupulously. When discussing the best patina for each bronze, Leonora used to say, 'It is the skin of these beings, they live through the colours that stain their bodies.' I remember a smelter bringing one of our sculptures back and being told by Leonora that he had to modify the figure's hat because the structure looked weak. I added that the toes lacked expression and tension, and this too weakened the object and diminished its vitality. The two of us would always alter details in this way, especially when the sculpture was in the plasticine stage. As we finished them, we chose what kind of patina we wanted.

The sculpture that demanded the most work was the one we called *The Magus*. The figure was a spell-maker, conjurer, enchanter, magician, necromancer. Leonora's 1945 painting *The Temptation of Saint Anthony* inspired the piece; she created this painting when she was already living in Mexico City. Every morning I would head

[48] Leonora Carrington and Gabriel Weisz, *The Dark Book* (Mexico: Tiempo Extra Editores, 1996).

to the smelter. I remember having to redo the lips to add more expression to the face. The moment Leonora set eyes on the sculpture, she knew we had to make the bronze express more movement because the character's tunic was flying in the wind. The founder wanted to carve the beard out of plasticine, but we decided that he should use wire instead. It would be difficult, because the sculpture is hollow; the workers had to pull each wire through the inside. The eyes had a green patina in contrast to the rest of the object, which was black. When Leonora and I were revising the bronze, she asked the founder to cut part of the tunic floating behind the figure. She wanted to reproduce *The Temptation of Saint Anthony* but knew that painting and sculpture are different representational languages; she, therefore, pointed out what belonged to the original painting but had to come off the sculpture. 'Don't you see, Gaby? The sculpture was too bulky and heavy. It's not necessary to include so much of the tunic here.' As a result, the sculpture ended up taking on a lightness and power that it had previously lacked. Leonora's ability to create a subtle balance between elements demonstrated a mastery of the form that has impressed many people. Each sculpture was a challenge – we had to visualise what is invisible in a painting, which is to say, the unperceived back side of a figure. One potential buyer complained about the green eyes, saying that they frightened her daughter and that she wanted them changed. I replied that she could always purchase a Disney toy from the market instead and stop pestering us. People often think about art as something ornamental, not understanding that certain figures require a poetic fierceness. Without it, the object would be weak and indifferent.

Among other bronze sculptures I worked on with Leonora was *Ask the Mask.* I remember the two of us standing looking at the sculpture and perceiving that there was something unsatisfactory about it, something missing. It was a bust with a half-moon face, but it looked flat and rigid to us. I said, 'How about pulling the horns back?' This curved the head. Leonora said, 'I dislike those lips.' So,

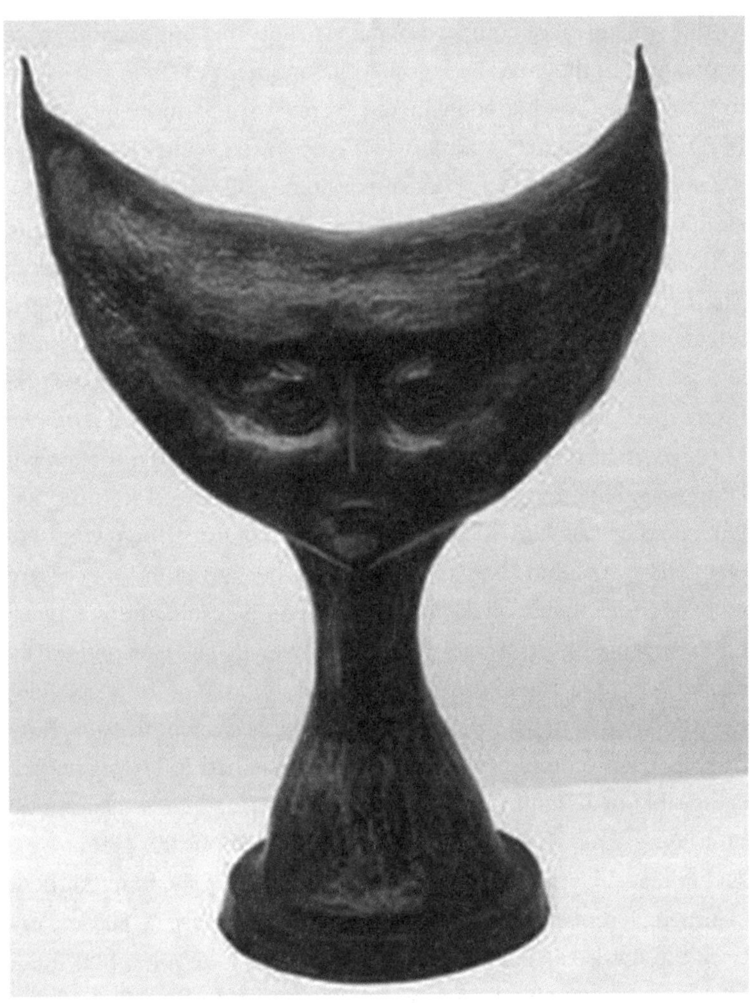

Leonora Carrington, *Ask the Mask*, 2008. Bronze sculpture, 100 × 70 × 30 cm.

we set to change those too. The sculpture was ready; it eventually acquired an impressive personality, somehow coming alive.

I wish that other sculptures that people erroneously attribute to Leonora had benefited from the same amount of critical examination. I have always admired the sculpture of a pig she made, which had a lid that turned it into a secret box. The original measurements were perfect. Some people have insisted on making them larger; the result is that the precise proportions are endangered. Each sculpture allows for a particular size. If one ignores the size, it loses its secret proportions and its volumetric meaning. None of them will tolerate monumentality. I remember when someone once asked for a lithograph, but we suggested a sculpture in small format instead; the piece turned into a dragon-bird. We worked the model in clay, which was taken to the kiln once it had hardened. When finished, it had a golden honey tone and red garnet stones for eyes. We called the piece *Sculpture-Vulture* (see Plate 13). We sent it to many Mexican embassies around the world. When Danny and I went to Dublin for an exhibition of Leonora's work, we found *Sculpture-Vulture* on display, years after they had exhibited this sculpture in the Library of México and the Museum of Modern Art in Mexico City.

We produced another piece which also originated in one of Leonora's paintings, this one titled *The Ancestor* (see Plate 14). It comprised a small scene set on a square onyx slate with four silver lemurs guarding the corners. The two of us decided to turn it into a ludic object, in which the silver creature in the middle can twirl around.

I remember my mother once saying to me, 'Come with me to the market.' We bought cheesecloth, chicken wire and carpenter's glue from the hardware store. The glue, which is a mixture of animal cartilage and bones, was left to soak overnight; this process goes back to ancient times. Then we put it in a bain-marie, at which point it began to emit a nauseating smell. Thereafter, Leonora began to bring to life a mysterious object that haunts every corner of the mind. What would the outcome be? First, she cut and shaped the chicken wire, then covered it with cheesecloth and a coat of the carpenter's glue, which becomes very hard and resistant when it is dry – for this reason Leonora often used this material. Leonora went out into the garden to fetch a dried rose stem, also destined to become part of this mysterious object, a kind of fetish. The next morning, we went

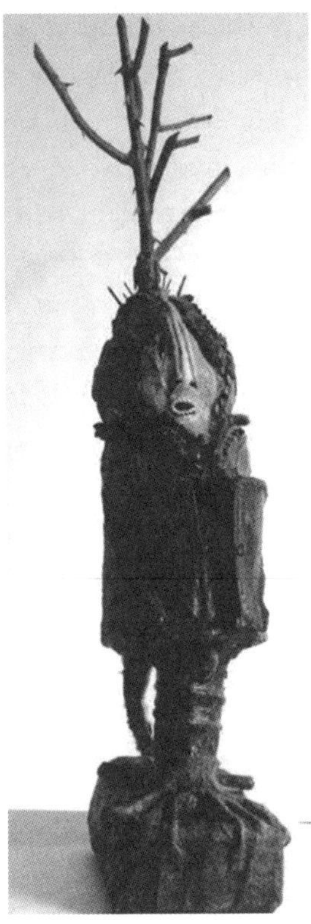

Leonora Carrington, *Fetish*, n.d. 66 × 12 cm.

to a costume jewellery shop where she chose two stones – people call them tiger eye stones; something tells me that the name inspires you – that were to serve as eyes. You also found some seeds and placed them around the eyes. These came from the Sonora market, also called the witches' market, where people bought remedies for a great variety of illnesses, including supernatural ones, as well as love charms and all sorts of other things. At the time several stands were guarded by taxidermy animals from the Natural History Museum. It was here, too, that we found a tail for our animal-sculpture, which was by this time rock solid because the glue had fully dried. The rose stem crowned its head, surrounded by little nails and some emerald scarabs. The fetish was hollow, and Leonora placed a small bag of stones inside it that also contained a glass ampoule like a retort, that instrument so crucial to an alchemist's laboratory, containing mercury, the legendary alchemical ingredient. This creature held the symbolic force of the Hermetic Tradition. Among her things, Leonora also found a single gold earring – its pair lost long ago – and incorporated it into the fetish. My inquisitive cat, puzzled by this strange collection of objects, tentatively inserted a paw into the hollow. Leonora also dipped some laces into the glue and formed them into spirals to create a pair of ears. Between its legs is a penis made from a curved seed, and a pair of beans to represent modest testicles. She painted different parts in white, grey, black, and brown. A tattoo runs down its back with an intense turquoise design in high relief, which she created from an acrylic paste often used to form decorative reliefs. She applied the mixture with a little spatula, and soon the fetish had the figure of a long creature running down its back. It was ready to guard the house.

I have mentioned already the ivory object that Leonora and I referred to as the White Goddess. One very hot evening in Italy, where I was participating in Eugenio Barba's theatre workshop, an event that took place in a former nuns' boarding school, after the day's activities I decided to take a shower, removing the White Goddess from around my neck and hanging her up before I did so. It wasn't until later, when I was fast asleep, dreaming about the Queen of Hearts from *Alice in Wonderland*, that I heard the Goddess screaming in indignation. I was suddenly wide awake, my hand flying to my chest where the White Goddess usually hangs and discovering she was missing. I rushed to the showers where I was relieved to find her hanging where I had left her. When, back in Mexico, I told Leonora about this peculiar adventure, she said, 'Objects have different ways of inhabiting our beings. But you should feel fortunate – you received a gift from your unconscious.'

Art, especially but not exclusively Surrealist art, can often be a kind of game. There was a playful element to Leonora's work, not only in her stories but also her paintings and the objects I

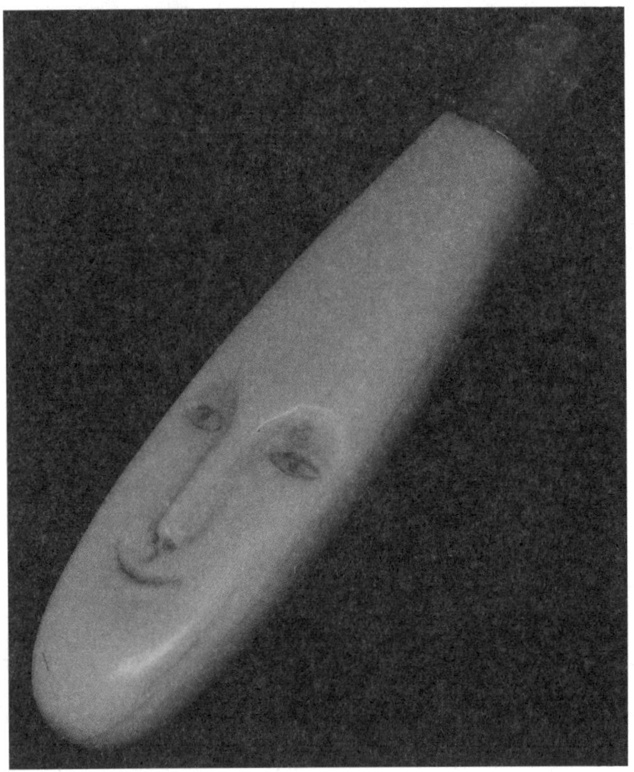

Leonora Carrington, *White Goddess*, n.d. Ivory pendant.

have mentioned here. I want to draw a connection between these anecdotes and a fairy tale by Hans Christian Andersen about a Chinese Emperor who prefers the tinkling sound of a mechanical nightingale, beautifully decorated with jewels, to the song of a real nightingale outside his window. The toy eventually breaks, however, and the Emperor falls critically ill, at which point the real nightingale comes out of the woods to bestow upon him his beautiful song. Death is so delighted by the sound that he agrees to prolong the Emperor's life.[49] Leonora had a particular liking for

[49] Hans Christian Andersen, 'The Nightingale' [Nattergalen], trans. Jean Hersholt, H. C. Andersen Centret, andersen.sdu.dk (accessed 12 February 2020).

this story, and I believe that most of her attraction to it stemmed from its poetic depiction of the mysterious appeal of both toys and animals. Every object she created had the same allure. A while ago, I came across some lines written by André Breton. He described dreaming about an object – a book, which depicted on its spine a wooden gnome with an Assyrian beard.[50] When he woke up, he was convinced of the book's existence and wanted to purchase it. Eventually he realised that the book existed only in his dreams. He did, however, always retain a close regard for that dream-object. This is the inverse experience to what happened to me with the White Goddess, a real object that appeared in a dream, revealing its oneiric life.

When Aggie and Pablito were small, Paty and I planned a picnic, which the children always loved. I was busy building a fire when two *campesinos* passed close by. We greeted them, and they went on their way. I carried on with what I was doing. Shortly after, however, the pair returned, mumbling 'Hands up!' The scene would have been comical if we hadn't feared for our children's lives – it so closely resembled one of those clichéd, terrible films in which a bad guy threatens the protagonist with a revolver. Paty was divested of her ring. 'Please, don't harm the girl', she said, as Aggie clung to her. So did Pablito, who she tried to calm as best she could. I was separated from my family at gunpoint and led away, where I was stripped of my ring and watch. The former was very dear to me – it had been a gift from Leonora, beautifully engraved and functioning also as a wax seal. All things considered, we were lucky to come out of the experience unharmed, though I was terribly sorry to lose the ring. An indescribable wound remains – something broken in human relations. Objects like that, which are stolen, or lost, or dreamed about, seem attached to our lives. Because we wear them,

---

[50] André Breton, quoted in Alina Clej, 'Phantoms of the Opera: Notes Toward a Theory of Surrealist Confession. The Case of Breton', *MLN*, 104.4 (1989), pp. 814–44 (820, n.).

they seem to have a story linked to our bodies, whether they are real or imaginary.

Of all these nostalgic stories, one, in particular, stands out for me. It concerns a small silver mask that never managed to come into being. Time and again Leonora and I tried to make alterations to the wax through a technique known to silversmiths as 'lost wax'. The problem was that the details were so fine that when the silver object came out of the cast, they were inevitably lost. We were repeatedly unsatisfied with the results, and ended up abandoning the project, which was a version of *Ask the Mask*, a bronze sculpture that I have already described. We were very disappointed not to be able to finish it. It is fascinating, though, to learn about different materials – to see results in silver, clay, or any other material. Leonora not only demonstrated mastery of these forms, but also proved herself to be an accomplished improviser, showing the dexterity and foresight to predict how materials would behave. Her hands could translate any material into whatever she wanted it to become.

I cannot avoid mentioning what happened to the sculptures attributed to Leonora after her death. I hate to think of those untalented thugs who abused her absence in order to promote a series of bronze monstrosities in her name. It is easy to see the creative weakness of these items sold and displayed in Mexico in comparison to the authentic sculptures produced by Leonora. You can feel the heavy-handedness of swindlers who tried but never succeeded in recreating her skill. The few sculptures she did create display elegance and artistic balance, qualities that are entirely lacking in those vulgar heaps of bronze, devoid of imagination as they are. I hate that these adulterations are being displayed all over the place, pretending to be authentic art, art that is being replaced by objects made by buffoons and self-promoters.

But enough now. Let's leave behind this horrible topic and move on to what Leonora wrote for the theatre. I still remember those sessions when we reworked *A Flannel Nightgown* together as an opera. We had lunch together every Tuesday, and for a while amused ourselves with this play, renamed *Crow Soup*, a sample of which was filmed and produced in Israel. When we thought some of the sections were too short, Leonora and I would walk into the characters as though they were chambers in a vast mansion. She already knew each of them intimately and invited me to join her with them.

'Do you agree that we should lead them to another place?'

'Yes', I replied. 'Let's invent other situations and conflicts for them, let us include different feelings.'

'What do you think about turning this character into one of those abominable adolescents?'

We laughed because we recalled some colourful individuals from our past.

Leonora even depicted a few of them in one of her paintings. I was there too, portrayed with a cigarette hanging from my lips in the company of no less sinister-looking types, one of whom was shooting a pistol at a gorgeous-looking pig. Over the next few lunches, we focused on *Crow Soup*, incorporating certain ideas I suggested, and then ran the whole thing through to see how it worked. It was like shaping a dramatic text sculpture with its own tones, rhythms, and even its own self-contained musical character.

*

It was not long before Chiki's sad demise. Thankfully, he died in his sleep, in his own home. His room was full of books, which in earlier years he had read so avidly, but which recently he had been deprived of by the cataracts that clouded his eyes. It upset me to see my father, once such an enthusiast for books, unable to do more than sit in front of the television and occasionally attempt a clumsy stroll around the house. Old age will reach us all, and we should be prepared for it, if at all possible. We will lose what we once were and enter into another stage of self. I have some difficulty walking these days, and I'm sure one day I'll eventually

walk as my father did in his final years. His burial had all the para-
phernalia of an orthodox Jewish ceremony. This was not my doing
and struck me as inappropriate, since Chiki never practised any
religion. What's more, Leonora and Paty were insulted when the
rabbi refused to shake hands with them. However, one tradition
forbids what another one doesn't. Chiki would never have agreed
to it, being an atheist. But when someone dies, people scurry out
of dark corners, feeling as though they have the right to impose
their conventions, the imposition of the coward. In death, we are
sequestered by the habits of others. There is an emptiness in my
stomach when I think of Chiki's final years. He left a long, solitary memory trail that visits me every now and then, like a ghost
haunting an old house, the kind of ghost that inhabits recollections, that emerges from mute photographs. One particular mental
vision comes to me: a train, like the one we once took in Europe.
Chiki is the sole passenger, his unmoving face looking out of the
window. It is night, and I have to shield myself from the icy wind.
I can make out his silhouette; he is standing up and wearing that
old heavy wool coat that was given to him by someone visiting
Mexico. I can see him because the train compartment is lit, but
he shows no sign of recognising me. Already in another planet of
mind and body.

When Leonora reached ninety, we celebrated by taking her
to San Diego. Paty had learned a couple of years before about a
group of people arguing over the seals that had recently 'colonised'
a beach known as the 'Children's Pool'. There was fierce debate
about whether to get rid of them or simply let them be. We took
Leonora to see them, and then arranged a visit to the zoo. Her love
of animals never disappeared from her stories, paintings, drawings, and tapestries, nor from any of the other materials she used
in her work (see Plate 15). They appeared in the form of mythical
creatures, visions of symbolic animals that allow us to be in touch
with the more enigmatic side of our selves. As I say this, I'll never
forget the time we went to the Chicago aquarium and Leonora

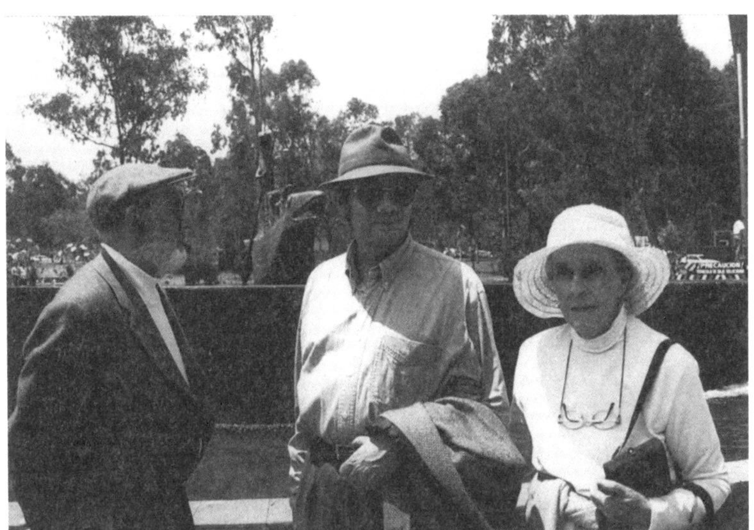

Chiki, Gabriel, and Leonora with the sculpture *Como hace el pequeño cocodrilo* (How does the little crocodile). Installed in Chapultepec, Mexico City, 2003.

remarked, 'seeing all these fish has sparked my appetite'. With that, the romanticised image of beautiful animals seen in simulations of their natural habitats came tumbling down. Leonora never lost her appreciation of irony, nor her iconoclastic, often black sense of humour. Animals were a means for her to understand her own animality, which is an important part of acquiring inner knowledge. This memory brings me to a moment when Daniel and I were look-ing at one of her ink drawings the other day, of a chained creature screaming with anguish and rage, which she created in response to how many of us felt during the awful political conditions of 1968. Like much of her work, this image of atavistic anger uses a spectral beast to visualise a powerful human emotion; animals and emo-tions are closely knit together.

On that trip to San Diego, Leonora was completely captivated by the plight of the seals, asking Paty time and time again what she had learned about the conflict over whether or not to let them settle in La Joya.

'Why don't they let them be?' Leonora asked.

'They complain that they smell and pollute the beach.'

Leonora looked at Paty, then pronounced: 'We humans smell worse, and they don't complain.' It goes without saying that Paty, Daniel, and I tried to protect the animals as best we could.

On our return to Mexico, Leonora showed me what turned out to be her last painting. It depicted a crow and a horse, with a lion underneath them and an old woman above, presiding over the animals with a contemplative expression. It's almost as though she is surveying her own existence. There is another woman beside her, and together the pair seem to be conjuring up a blue creature visible behind them. A wordless and timeless communication seems to embrace both women. It is a painting of old age. There's something peaceful about it; the kind of peacefulness you want to inhabit at the end of your life, although it is spiced with a bit of danger too (see Plate 16).

Every Tuesday, when Leonora and I had lunch together in Mexico, she would ask, 'What's going on in the world?' I never quite felt ready to answer, because so many things happen in a week. I would choose a couple, describing them slowly, aware that my mother was becoming more and more distant from the world she was soon to leave. I can see her sitting in a large room, inhabiting, it seems, that indefinable territory of old age. She fell down a staircase and fractured her cheekbone and eye socket. I took her to the hospital and sat on a chair outside her room all night long, unable to enter because she was in intensive care. An internist came out of the room at one point, barely able to stop laughing. Paty asked why he was so amused, and he said, 'Leonora insisted on having a smoke. I explained that that wasn't possible, it would be dangerous because of the oxygen tank, but she just said: "Look, let's make a deal, if you allow me to smoke, I will paint something for you."' The young doctor confessed, chortling, that the temptation to accept was there.

I was in San Diego, visiting Danny at university when I got a call from Paty saying that I ought to return to Mexico because Leonora's health had deteriorated, and this might be the end. Leonora was, by this point, mostly silent. She gave us one final gift of a painting – an invisible one, one that never came to fruition: she pointed at the whitewashed wall, and when I asked her what she was looking at so intently, she replied, 'There are some black birds circling there. Can't you see them?' That wall in her home will always be marked, for me, by that final imaginary painting.

In Leonora's final months, both Pablo and Daniel read her the stories she wrote for me when I was an infant, and which I read to all my children too. She found it difficult to sit up, now that she was so weak, but sometimes she was aware of her surroundings and smiled as my sons read to her. Eventually, both of them would have to return to the US, but Paty and I began the work of soothing her and gradually letting go. On one visit I read her a poem by Ezra Pound. She hadn't uttered a word for several days, but on hearing it, she suddenly opened her mouth to complain: 'I didn't like that at all, what you just read.' Each day I tried reading something different – including *Alice in Wonderland*. Carroll was always one of her favourite authors, so no complaints there. Remembering how impressed she used to be by *The Tibetan Book of the Dead*, and how many conversations we had had about it, I read her a whole series of passages from that, too. It acts as a kind of somatic metaphor, I think, warning the body about the obstacles we confront so fearfully, about the work of achieving a good death. If death is a kind of blindness, what a wonderful idea is to have a narrative that we can follow in *The Tibetan Book of the Dead* as we are near to the end.[51]

My time with her was brutally interrupted when they admitted her to hospital. I went with her in the ambulance – a terrifying journey, since so few people on the streets were willing to let us pass.

---

[51] W. Y. Evans-Wentz (ed.), *The Tibetan Book of the Dead or the After-Death Experiences on the Bardo Plane, according to Lāma Kazi Dawa-Samdup's English Rendering*, 2nd edn (London: Oxford University Press, 1949).

When we arrived, Leonora had a respirator which from then on she wore both day and night. The hospital's medical regime of terror had begun. Paty and I took turns to stay with her overnight. Paty reminded me that she had asked, once, whether Leonora feared death, and my mother had replied: 'Not death, no. I fear old age.' I tried to reason with the doctor, asking him not to prolong her agony. Extending her life was both selfish and cruel at this point.

I will never forget the phone call I got from Paty in the middle of the night, telling me to get to the hospital as soon as I could. I nearly crashed the car as I accidentally careered into the pavement. I felt sick, scarcely able to breathe, panic crawling over my entire body.

Leonora had already passed away when I arrived at the hospital. I am glad that Paty was with her. Her benevolent and loving presence will have been a comfort. Leonora's death was a catastrophe; I have lost a friend, an accomplice in my creative adventures. I am unable to express this loss. The light of memory dims, and the great manner of being is turned off. You are gone. This text is a work of grief and a final farewell.

ACKNOWLEDGEMENTS

This book would not have been possible without the support and encouragement of my editor, Emma Brennan, and her assistant, Alun Richards, who read the manuscript and made very useful suggestions. A grateful acknowledgement is also due to my friend Jonathan Eburne for his kind and intelligent preface. I appreciate all the help Maria Fernanda Pessaro at the Artists Rights Society in New York has offered for this book. I am also indebted to Paul de Angelis who so kindly put me in contact with Emma Brennan.

I am especially grateful for the encouragement from my wife, Martha Patricia, my sons, Daniel and Pablo, and my daughter, Agatha. In particular, I want to thank my wife, who was patient enough to read the manuscript, and Daniel for his recommendations and special research. I also want to thank the late Leonora for the conversations we shared, for the gift of collaborating with me on a number of artistic projects, and above all for her exceptional life's work – it is an extraordinary legacy to leave behind for all of humanity. I am also grateful to my father for all our long conversations and for his book recommendations, and to Joanna Moorhead, who gave me access to correspondence from my grandmother during the war. I also want to thank Paul de Angelis, the former editor of Leonora's books, who gave us a whole box of my mother's documents when we visited his house in Connecticut. Finally, I am indebted to Cynthia Young for sharing correspondence that alluded to my father's detention by the French fascists in Morocco and his arrival in Mexico.

SELECT BIBLIOGRAPHY

I present here a list of correspondence, notes and interviews that were used in the research for this memoir and from which certain ideas and statements derive.

ABRAHAMS, C., and C. G. Montefiore, *The Jewish Quarterly Review*, XI (New York: Macmillan, 1899).

ANDERSEN, Hans Christian, 'The Nightingale' [Nattergalen], trans. Jean Hersholt, H. C. Andersen Centret, andersen.sdu.dk (accessed 12 February 2020).

CARRINGTON, Leonora, 'La Dame Ovale', illustrations by Max Ernst (Guy Lévis Mano, 1939).

_______ *Down Below*, intro. Marina Warner (New York: New York Review of Books, 2017).

_______ *En bas*, ed. Henri Parisot, Collection L'Age D'or (Paris: Fontaine, 1945).

_______ 'Penélope', manuscript in personal archive.

_______ *The Seventh Horse and Other Tales*, trans. Katherine Talbot and Anthony Kerrigan (New York: Dutton, 1988).

CARRINGTON, Leonora, and Gabriel Weisz, *The Dark Book*, etchings, aquatint and texts (Mexico: Tiempo Extra Editores, 1996).

CARTER, William, *Preservation Hall: Music from the Heart* (London: Cassell, 1991).

CHARRIÈRE, Christian, 'Review of *Pénélope*', *Docsur: Documents sur le surréalisme*, 1 (1986).

CLEJ, Alina, 'Phantoms of the Opera: Notes Toward a Theory of Surrealist Confession. The Case of Breton', *MLN*, 104.4 (1989), pp. 814–44.

DAUMAL, René, *Mount Analogue: An Authentic Narrative*, trans. Roger Shattuck (San Francisco: City Lights, 1969 [1952]).

EMERTON, J. A., 'Yahweh and his Asherah: The Goddess or her Symbol?', *Vetus Testamentum*, 49.3 (1999), pp. 315–37, www.jstor.com/stable/1585374 (accessed 9 September 2020).

EVANS-WENTZ, W. Y. (ed.), *The Tibetan Book of the Dead or the After-*

Death Experiences on the Bardo Plane, according to Lāma Kazi Dawa-Samdup's English Rendering, 2nd edn (London: Oxford University Press, 1949).

FIGURA, Starr, 'Diego Rivera's "The Communicating Vessels"', *Print Quarterly*, 13.4 (1996), pp. 413–15, www.jstor.org/stable/41824953 (accessed 26 March 2020).

FOWLES, John, *The Magus* (New York: Dell, 1983 [1965]).

HEFFERNAN, Claire, 'Tibetan Veterinary Medicine', *Nomadic Peoples*, 1.2 (1997), pp. 37–54, www.jstor.org/stable/43123525 (accessed 9 April 2020).

JAMES, Edward, 'Preface' to Leonora's exhibition at Pierre Matisse Gallery, New York, 1948, personal archives.

JEAN, Marcel, *The Autobiography of Surrealism: The Documents of Twentieth-Century Art* (New York: Viking Press, 1980).

LEARY, Timothy, Ralph Metzner and Richard Alpert, 'Tibetan Manual for Ego-transcendent Experience Using Psychedelic Substances', in *Psychedelic Monograph No. 2*, 3rd edn (Zihuatanejo, México, 1962; Antigua: I.F.I.T, 1963).

LEBRUN, Bernard, and Unidad Lefebvre, *Robert Capa: The Paris Years 1933–1954*, trans. Nicholas Elliot (New York: Abrams, 2012).

LONG, Asphodel P., 'Asherah, the Tree of Life and the Menorah: Continuity of a Goddess Symbol in Judaism?', The First Sophia Fellowship Feminist Theology Lecture, College of St Mark & St John, Plymouth, 4 December 1996, www.grayish.demon.co.uk/bisft/Asherah.pdf (accessed 9 September 2020).

MINDELL, Arnold, *Dreambody: The Body's Role in Revealing the Self*, ed. Sisa Sternback, Scott and Becky Goodman, intro. Marie-Louise von Franz (Santa Monica, CA: Sigo Press, 1982).

El mundo mágico de los Mayas, Instituto Nacional de Antropología e Historia, 1st edn (Ciudad de México: SEP, 1964).

PAUWELS, Louis (ed.), *Monsieur Gurdjieff: Documents, témoinages, textes et commentaires sur une société initiatique contemporaine* (Paris: Seuil, 1954).

RUBEL, Arthur J., et al., *Susto, a Folk Illness* (Berkeley, CA: University of California Press, 1984).

SAMTEN, Karmay G., *The Treasury of Good Sayings: A Tibetan History of Bon* (Oxford: Oxford University Press, 1972).

SCHOLEM, Gershom, *Major Trends in Jewish Mysticism* (New York: Schocken, 1954 [1946]).

SOLDNER, Paul, 'The Fantastic Palace of Ferdinand Cheval', *Craft Horizons*, 28.1 (1968), pp. 9–19.

SOUTHERN, J. Mark, and David Goldfield (eds), *New Orleans on Parade: Tourism and the Transformation of the Crescent City* (Baton Rouge, LA: Louisiana State University Press, 2006).

VARO, Remedios, *Cartas, sueños y otros textos*, ed. Isabel Castells (Tlaxcala: Era, 1994).

YOUNG, Cynthia (ed.), *The Mexican Suitcase: Spanish Civil War Negatives of Capa, Chim and Taro*, International Centre of Photography (New York: Steidel, 2010).

ILLUSTRATIONS

Plates

1   The wooden door painted by Leonora Carrington at the house
    where she lived with Max Ernst in St Martin d'Ardèche, France.
    © 2020 Estate of Leonora Carrington / Artists Rights Society (ARS),
    New York.

2   Max Ernst, *Leonora in the Morning Light*, 1940. Oil on canvas, 66 ×
    82 cm. © 2020 Artists Rights Society (ARS), New York / VG Bild-
    Kunst, Bonn.

3   Leonora Carrington, screen, 1964. Oil on wood, 114 × 45 cm. © 2020
    Estate of Leonora Carrington / Artists Rights Society (ARS), New York.

4   Leonora Carrington, *Crookhey Hall*, 1947. Casein on Masonite,
    31 × 60 cm. © 2020 Estate of Leonora Carrington / Artists Rights
    Society (ARS), New York.

5   Leonora Carrington, *Habdalah Asejaledha*, 1959. Oil on canvas,
    65.5 × 113 cm. © 2020 Estate of Leonora Carrington / Artists Rights
    Society (ARS), New York.

6   Leonora Carrington, *Sisters of the moon, Lucienne*, 1932.
    Watercolour, ink and graphite on paper. © 2020 Estate of Leonora
    Carrington / Artists Rights Society (ARS), New York.

7   Leonora Carrington, *Las serpientes*, 1961. Wool and gold thread.
    254 × 110 cm. © 2020 Estate of Leonora Carrington / Artists Rights
    Society (ARS), New York.

8   Leonora Carrington, *Seraputina's Rehearsal*, 1947. Casein on
    Masonite, 60 × 50 cm. © 2020 Estate of Leonora Carrington / Artists
    Rights Society (ARS), New York.

9   Leonora Carrington, *El mundo mágico de los Mayas*, 1963. Casein on
    board, 200 × 431 cm. © 2020 Estate of Leonora Carrington / Artists
    Rights Society (ARS), New York.

10 Leonora Carrington, *Master Dragonfly*, 1975. Humorous diploma
    for Gabriel Weisz. Casein on parchment. © 2020 Estate of Leonora
    Carrington / Artists Rights Society (ARS), New York.

Figures